The
Inward
Pilgrimage

An Introduction to
Christian Spiritual
Classics

The
Inward
Pilgrimage

An Introduction to

Christian Spiritual

Classics

Bernhard Christensen

Foreword by Bradley P. Holt

Augsburg

MINNEAPOLIS

To Gracia
and to Nadia, Marya, Marina, and Sonya
and in memory of Naomi

THE INWARD PILGRIMAGE
An Introduction to Christian Spiritual Classics

Revised edition. First published by Augsburg Publishing House in 1976.

Cover and text design by David Meyer

Library of Congress Cataloging-in-Publication Data

Christensen, Bernhard M. (Bernhard Marinus), 1901–1984.
    The inward pilgrimage : an introduction to Christian spiritual classics / Bernhard M. Christensen. — Rev. ed.
        p. cm.
    Includes bibliographical references.
    ISBN 0-8066-2036-6 (alk. paper)
    1. Christian literature—History and criticism. 2. Spirituality—History. I. Title.
BR117.C47   1996
248—dc20   95-53694
                                                                              CIP

The paper used in this publication meets the minimum requirements of American National Standard for Information Sciences—Permanence of Paper for Printed Library Materials, ANSI Z329.48-1984.   ●

Manufactured in the U.S.A.   AF 9-2036

00   99   98   97   96   2   3   4   5   6   7   8   9   10

Contents

Foreword

The book you hold in your hand is designed to guide pilgrims on their spiritual journey. It surveys the landscape of Christian tradition, identifying the major mountains and rivers, and cathedrals and castles, which the reader is invited to explore.

This book impressed the people who already knew that landscape very well when it was first published twenty years ago. Dr. Coleman Barry, a noted Roman Catholic educator, wrote, "Dr. Christensen's choice of the primary sources and his own deeply spiritual interpretations of them, provide us with a rare overview of Western Christian interior life." A prominent Quaker scholar, Dr. Elton Trueblood, remarked, "We have had several studies of the classics of Christian devotion in our century, but none surpasses that of Bernhard Christensen. His scope is wide and his penetration is deep."

These men, and much of their generation, have died. But with the re-issuing of *The Inward Pilgrimage* a new generation of readers is now invited, in Christensen's words, to "a walk through the centuries in the company of good friends of God." Who is the man who offers to guide us on this walk? Bernhard Christensen (1901–1984) was a gifted student, beloved professor, and honored president at Augsburg College in Minneapolis. Although he finished both seminary and doctoral programs in theology, he chose not to be ordained. His ability to use historical and philosophical tools in thinking through the great issues of our time were well demonstrated, but his greatest love was for those who heroically *lived* the Christian faith.

Although Christensen was a lifelong member of a very small church body, the Lutheran Free Church, he developed a wide ecumenical vision that included the Eastern Orthodox, Roman Catholic, Pentecostal, Protestant, Evangelical, and other traditions. His attendance at the founding assembly of the World Council of Churches in 1948 helped him to see the Christian fellowship in a broad, global perspective. In this and other ways he was far ahead of his time.

Christensen struggled with many obstacles; his was not the life of a holy recluse. The responsibilities of administration were thrust upon him, as upon many others earlier in church history. After serving for a quarter century as the chief executive of a small college constantly in need of funds, he retired with the hope of writing and teaching at

Luther Seminary in St. Paul. Those hopes were challenged by serious health problems and limited mobility. Bernhard and his wife, Lilly Gracia, experienced the grief of their daughter Naomi's death and the grief of his illness, but together they persevered in writing this book. Its diction and style owe much to her gifts, also expressed as a professor of English.

The Inward Pilgrimage was Christensen's last book, the ripened legacy of a deep spirit and brilliant mind. His love of literature and his delight in discovering women and men who live out Christian spirituality come together in this volume. Some of the books discussed here are well known, but others will be new discoveries for most readers. All will illustrate distinctive styles of Christian life, invitations to the reader to find among the many-splendorous ways of love that unique path to which God is calling.

The wide distribution of the first edition of this book testifies to the fact that it is not only a stepping stone to the classics of Christian spirituality, but is itself a classic in the life of the Spirit. Bernhard Christensen read widely and deeply; his comments on these books show his own sensitivity to the moving of God in the great writers. He belongs among them.

And so, to you the reader comes the opportunity to meet this deep spirit through his enthusiasm for these books and his evaluations of them. I know from personal experience that if you could converse with him, he would challenge you to find the truth of the spiritual life by experiencing it. Books are important means for one soul to speak to another, but they are only the means and not the end. These books can suggest possibilities you may never have considered and encourage you or rebuke you on the way. But it is for you to discover your path, your castle, your cathedral, and to find there both yourself and the loving mystery of God in Jesus Christ.

BRADLEY P. HOLT, 1995

Prologue

"There is a river whose streams make glad the city of God." This beautiful metaphor from Psalm 46 suggests the place of the spiritual classics in the life of the Christian church. Arising in many ages and many lands, these writings nourish the Christian as a clear-flowing stream nourishes the trees along its banks. Offering life-giving spiritual food, they truly "make glad" the hearts of those who dwell in the city of God.

But what is a spiritual classic—or, to use a more familiar term, a devotional classic? How do a few books, from among the thousands of religious books ever written, come to have this singular distinction? All spiritual classics seem to have at least five essential characteristics in common:

1. First of all, they are not concerned basically with doctrine or ethics, but instead with the person's life with God. Their chief aim is not to instruct the mind but to lift the heart toward the Eternal.

2. They have stood the test of time, having been read and loved without losing their appeal.

3. They are ecumenical in outlook, appealing to Christians of many times and many denominations. Each book reflects its own age and circumstances of writing, yet to a remarkable degree speaks to the condition of Christians everywhere.

4. They deal especially with the great theme of prayer, so central to all religious experience. As Douglas Steere, well-known author of books on the inner life, has said,

> Nearly all these great books relate themselves to prayer. They lead up to prayer, they make prayer necessary, they almost force us into prayer. . . . [They] touch upon the areas of life that prayer deals with.[1]

5. Finally, they are books not to be read once and laid aside but instead to be reread and meditated upon. They are not passing acquaintances but abiding companions on the way of life.

Every age of the church has produced examples of these treasures of spirituality. With the passage of time, however, and with the rise of divisions within the church, even some of the finest of the classics have come to be neglected. A major purpose of this book is to introduce today's reader to a number of the greatest classics portraying the "inward pilgrimage." The ones presented here are but a few, yet a chosen few, with representation from each of three epochs of the church's history: ancient, medieval, and modern. Since it is the author's hope that reading this volume will be a stepping-stone to reading the classics themselves, I have chosen books that are readily available—in most instances in paperback editions. Judged by the five criteria listed above, these sixteen books are all worthy of being known by Christians of all denominations.

What greater reading privilege could there be, aside from reading the Scriptures themselves, than to share in the companionship of those through whom we have been given so rich a spiritual endowment? If it is a good thing to cultivate the fellowship of contemporary spiritual Christians, it is an equal enrichment, by means of the printed page, to "walk through the centuries" in the company of good friends of God.

Such a walk leads inevitably to the vision of the manifold variety of spiritual experience. As the colors of one spectrum of light can blend into numberless patterns of beauty, so the one light of faith reveals itself in a multitude of life patterns, all beautiful. The gifts and graces of the Spirit have come to expression in widely different forms in different ages of the church, but an essential unity pervades them all. The piety of an English Baptist differs from that of a Scandinavian Lutheran; a North American Quaker's prayer life will not be the same as that of a Spanish Catholic. Yet the divergent patterns of faith all reflect the one life in Christ. And learning to know the spiritual life as it has been lived among men and women of other cultures and other churches can add immeasurably to our own inward pilgrimage.

Furthermore, these books have a vital contribution to make to our practical life day by day. In *As the Spirit Leads Us*, Dorothy Ranaghan describes the aim of Christian spirituality as "a plan, a means, an attempt to find a way of living every day in a growing union with God."[2] The spiritual classics, while building upon the enduring realities of the Christian faith, will give such guidance. Although some were written centuries ago, they still speak to our needs today.

Although these classics do not all stress with equal emphasis our participation in the life and activities of the church, they also do not foster spiritual individualism. The "life together," portrayed by Dietrich Bonhoeffer, is clearly rooted in the Word and the Sacraments. St. Francis seeks the approbation of his bishop. The Russian pilgrim attends the public liturgy at every possible opportunity. The spiritual classics, rightly read, will lead us closer to the heart of the church, to its worship and sacraments, and to its fellowship and worldwide mission.

Finally, to read the spiritual classics is to explore the "mansions within," so well described by St. Teresa of Avila in *The Interior Castle*. Her "mansions" are arranged in a definite order of spiritual progression, but the spirituality unveiled in the classics depicts the soul at many levels, often with no attempt at structural portrayal. From its own unique approach, each book reflects and illuminates the inward pilgrimage and urges readers themselves to enter into a quest of a fuller life with God.

Each chapter in this book seeks to characterize the spiritual setting in which a particular classic originated, to give a vignette of the author's life, and to summarize the main teachings of the book, including representative quotations. *The Inward Pilgrimage* aims primarily to be a helpful introduction before reading of the masterpieces themselves. At the same time, it is the author's hope that the reading of these chapters will in itself be a meaningful devotional experience, and that it may lead to reading and discussing the classics with others—seekers, friends, and kindred spirits. For spiritual truth is most fully possessed only when it is passed on.

THE SETTING: 4th-century North Africa and Italy
THE BOOK: A renowned Church Father reflects on the transforming grace
of God and our unending quest for truth

1

The Confessions

St. Augustine

*I wandered upon the broad way of the world,
but you did not forsake me.*

The Confessions of St. Augustine, one of the greatest autobiographies in history, is also one of the most widely known and loved of all Christian books. Written about a dozen years after its author's conversion to the Christian faith, it tells the story of his childhood and youth, his early departure into a life of sin, his years of philosophical searching, and his gradual return to God and to inner peace. In form, the book is one continuous heart-searching prayer, as the author bares his soul to God and to his readers. He quotes the Scriptures constantly but also draws upon the wisdom of secular literature and philosophy, both fields in which he was well schooled. Abounding in passages of keen intellectual analysis and profound spiritual insight, *The Confessions* portrays both the depths and the heights of human experience. "No writer," says John K. Ryan, "ever went deeper into his own character and deeds, passed keener judgments upon himself, or revealed himself more fully and more humbly to others."[1]

At the same time, *The Confessions* is a continuous hymn of praise to the glory of the Creator and Redeemer of humankind. Its eloquent presentation of Christian truth and of the soul's longing for God has been likened to great organ music; and like great music the book can be heard, or read, again and again, ever opening new vistas of beauty and meaning.

Aurelius Augustine was born in Tagaste in north Africa in A.D. 354. His mother, Monica, was a Christian, but his father was not. Augustine was not baptized as a child, but his mother's prayers surrounded him from his birth. Nevertheless, his years of childhood and youth were unhappy. Looking back upon them, he recalls the unreasonableness and cruelty of his teachers, his utter distaste for some of the subjects he was forced to study, his yielding to temptations such as stealing—just "for the fun of it" or from fear of his companions' ridicule. His parents showed more concerned for the development of his brilliant mind than for the formation of his character. Lacking inward stability and surrounded by temptations, Augustine rapidly degenerated.

The Confessions shows that even during these bitter years, however, there were glimpses of light, upward urgings, deep dissatisfactions. His reading of *Hortensius* by Cicero awakened a thirst for true wisdom, which never left him. Despite his moral aberrations, he became a teacher of rhetoric at a young age. But he was not at peace. For years he went from one philosophy to another. Manichaeism, a dualistic religion that exalted both God and evil, held him captive for years but lost its hold upon him when one of its leading teachers proved to be inwardly shallow. For a time he was allured by astrology, but the counsel of a good physician friend liberated him from that snare. The teachings of the Platonists were helpful, but not enough to give him the peace he desired.

Gradually his mind and heart were drawn back toward Christianity. When he began to study the Christian doctrines in earnest, he found himself at first both attracted and repelled. On the one hand, he felt that the simplicity of the Scriptures could not compare to the nobility of Cicero's style and thought. And yet, he writes, he saw

> something within them that was neither revealed to the proud nor made plain to children, that was lowly on one's entrance but lofty on further advance, and that was veiled over in mysteries.[2]

The Scriptures seemed to call for a childlike spirit, whereas he disdained the idea of being a little child. And always his sensual sins held him fast. He had lived with a concubine for years, and he could not bear the thought of giving her up. Sometimes he prayed, "Make me pure— but not yet!" Little by little the vanity and emptiness of the world's wisdom became clear to him:

> What did it profit me that I, who was then a most wicked servant of base lusts, should read and understand all the books of the liberal arts? . . . I found joy in these books, but I did not know the source of whatever was good and certain within them. I had my back to the light.[3]

When he was about thirty years old, Augustine, weary of the disreputable conduct of his students in Carthage, went to Rome. But teaching there presented other irritating problems, so after a short time he accepted a position in Milan. His mother and some of his friends accompanied him.

In Milan he came under the influence of the great Bishop Ambrose, whose example and preaching came to be of critical importance in Augustine's life. He was challenged by the bishop's noble life and by his continence. The sermons of Ambrose were of particular help in clearing away many false interpretations of Scripture. "The letter kills, but the spirit gives life," he would constantly emphasize, as he showed that a great deal of the Bible was to be understood spiritually and not literally.

As Augustine listened, his mind was convinced. But as we read of his conversion experience in *The Confessions*, we see that his heart ultimately found rest not through human philosophy or learning, not even through the arguments of persuasive preaching, but through personal contacts with people with a living faith in Christ. But first both his mind and heart had to be convinced of the central message of the gospel.

> I sought for a way of gaining strength sufficient for me to have joy in you, but I did not find it until I embraced the mediator between God and man, the man Christ Jesus, who is over all things, God blessed forever.[4]

Acceptance of the Incarnation became the key to the door of faith into which he was soon to be ushered by the voice of a little child.

Some months after coming to Milan, Augustine—deeply aware of his need of spiritual counsel—sough out Simplicianus, an older Christian who was also a friend of Bishop Ambrose. From Simplicianus he learned the story of Victorinus, a great pagan teacher who in his old age became a Christian and made public the conversion of his faith. As Augustine listened to this story about Victorinus, he says, "I was on fire to imitate him." But he did not yet make the crucial decision. He was still, as he says, "in both caps," likening himself to a man beginning to be awakened from sleep, who says drowsily, "Let me be for a while longer."

Then one day a visitor, a fellow African named Ponticianus, came to the home of Augustine and his friend Alypius. Ponticianus was a Christian, and when he noticed a volume of the epistles of St. Paul lying there, he was led to tell how two friends of his had been converted through reading the life of St. Anthony the hermit. As Augustine heard how Anthony had forsaken all to live a life of utter devotion to God in the desert, he was deeply moved. When Ponticianus left, his heart was in a torment of indecision, torn between the call of sensuality and the call of God. Leaving Alypius, he went out into the garden adjoining the house and wept bitterly.

Suddenly, in a moment of silence, he heard the voice of a child in an adjacent yard repeating the words, "Take up and read; take up and read." It seemed to him that God was speaking directly to him. Here are Augustine's words describing what followed:

> I hurried back to the spot where Alypius was sitting, for I had put there the volume of the apostle when I got up and left him. I snatched it up, opened it, and read in silence the chapter on which my eye first fell: "Not in rioting and drunkenness, not in clambering and impurities, not in strife and envying; but put you on the Lord Jesus Christ, and make no provisions for the flesh, in it concupiscence." No further wished I to read, nor was there need to do so. Instantly, in truth, at the end of this sentence, as if before a peaceful light streaming into my heart, all the dark shadows of doubt fled away.[5]

The story of Augustine's conversion is recorded in Book 8 of *The Confessions*. For him it marked the great transition from death to life. Now a new life opened. Book 9 tells how he resigned his professorship, how with a group of friends he spent some months in study, how at

Easter in A.D. 387 he was baptized by Bishop Ambrose together with his son Adeodatus and with Alypius, and how together with his mother and his brother he journeyed to Rome enroute to his home in Africa. Monica's prayers for her son had been more than answered. Now she was ready to bid farewell to this earth. "What am I doing here any longer?" she asked.

Before telling of his mother's death, Augustine pays beautiful tribute to her as both a faithful wife and a devoted mother. He speaks to God about her, calling her "that handmaiden of yours who brought me to birth, both in her flesh so that I was born into this temporal light, and in her heart, that I might be born into eternal light."[6] He tells of her great patience in the hardships and wrongs she suffered at the hands of her husband, whom she at last won to Christ; and of her consecrated life as the "servant of the servants of God." Gratefully he points to the secret of her noble life: "She had you," he says to God, "as her inward teacher in the school of the heart."[7]

One of the most beautiful passages in *The Confessions*, and indeed in all religious literature, is Augustine's account of his conversation with his mother shortly before her death, as they stood by a window looking out over a garden in Ostia. They speak of the meaning of "eternal life," the life set free from all the burdens and shadows of time. As they converse, they rise ever higher in thought and spirit, until, as it were, they are in the very presence of the Eternal. It is not strange that Monica was ready to bid earth farewell. Earlier she had wanted to be buried by her husband in Africa, but now she simply said, "Nothing is far from God."[8]

Books 8 and 9, where Augustine describes personally and in detail the central crisis of his life, are no doubt the most fascinating parts of *The Confessions*, but the entire work is a treasure chest of spiritual truth and insight. The whole story of Augustine's long pilgrimage from sin and doubt to purity and faith is filled with examples and precepts for every Christian. The last part of *The Confessions* (Books 10 to 13), dealing chiefly with intricate philosophical and theological problems, is perhaps less helpful to most readers.

The record of the last half of Augustine's long life until his death in A.D. 430—as bishop of Hippo, as scholar and writer, as fearless conversationalist and gentle pastor of his people—all of this lies beyond the scope of *The Confessions*. But the book still remains the best introduction to the greatest of the Western church fathers and among all these writings is the most direct source of spiritual help for the lay reader. Almost every page of *The Confessions* abounds in words of wisdom that have been the inspiration of Christians ever since they were first written. Many passages deserve not only to be mediated upon, but also to be made a permanent treasure of our hearts. Who among all earth's writers can speak as eloquently and profoundly as St. Augustine on the greatest themes: God and humanity, life and death, sin and grace, time and eternity? Once read and pondered, passages like the following can scarcely be forgotten:

> You have made us for yourself, O Lord, and our heart is restless until it rests in you.[9]

> Give what you command, and command what you will.[10]

> Too narrow is the house of my soul for you to enter into it: let it be enlarged by you. It lies in ruins; build it up again.[11]

> Too late have I loved you, O Beauty so ancient and new, too late have I loved you! Behold, you were within me while I was outside: it was there that I sought you, and rushed headlong upon these things of beauty which you have made. You were with me, but I was not with you. They kept me far from you, those fair things which, if they were not in you, would not exist at all. You have called to me and have cried out, and have shattered my deafness. You have blazed forth with light, . . . and have put my blindness to flight. . . . I have tasted you and I hunger and thirst after you. You have touched me, and I have burned for your peace.[12]

> Wheresoever I found truth, there I found my God, truth itself.[13]

The Confessions, which begins by praising God's greatness and God's gifts, closes with a sublime prayer for the greatest gift of all, that the peace of God, "the peace without an evening," may be ours forever:

> O Lord God, give us peace, for you have given all things to us, the peace of rest, the peace of the sabbath, the peace without an evening. This entire most beautiful order of things that are very good . . . is to pass

away. For truly in them a morning has been made and an evening also. But the seventh day is without an evening, because you have sanctified it to endure to all eternity. . . . We also, after our works, . . . may rest in you in the sabbath of eternal life.

Then also you shall rest in us, even as now you work in us, and so will that rest of yours be in us. . . . But you, O Lord, are ever at work and ever at rest.[14]

It is a high vision of human destiny to come to the soul of a man— a vision of unending fellowship with the living God, he in us and we in him; and we, in whom he has worked here in our earth years, now become also the place of his eternal rest. The storms of sin and the tempests of time are past. The Lord God Omnipotent— the Lord of Omnipotent Love—reigneth, forever and ever!

2

The Desert Fathers

Helen Waddell

*Their denial of the life of earth has been
the incalculable enriching of it.*

One of the strangest movements in the entire history of Christendom was the flight of tens of thousands of Christians during the fourth and fifth centuries into the hermit life of the deserts of Egypt and the Near East. There they lived in solitude or in small groups, with only the barest necessities of life, and spent their time chiefly in prayer and in an earnest quest for a deeper life with God. When we read of them, we may at first be tempted to turn away in utter disbelief, even in disgust, thinking that the whole movement was mere fanaticism. But if we pause to become better acquainted with these desert-dwellers, their ways and their wisdom, their defeats and their victories, we find that they have something of unique and enduring worth to say to us.

Such a closer acquaintance has been made possible through the publication of *The Desert Fathers*, by Helen Waddell, an English classical and medieval scholar. By careful editing of selected passages chosen from the masses of material that have been preserved, and with the addition of helpful notes, the author opens the door for today's readers to enter into a "fellowship of solitude" with these men and women of long ago. In addition to these solitaries of the wilderness, Waddell introduces a number of other striking figures, not strictly hermits but also people exhibiting a similar spirit of discipline and great gentleness. Included too are the stories of a number of women redeemed from sin through the witness of the saintly hermits. The desert scene was stern and unrelenting, but in its midst blossomed memorable flowers of grace and virtue.

St. Antony of Egypt, though not the first hermit, set the pattern and drew multitudes of other men and women to the desert. Noted historian Edward Gibbon called Antony's life and influence a vast tragedy—but there was in Anthony's work value that historians can overlook.

Anthony was born in Coma in upper Egypt in about the year 251. His parents were wealthy, earnest Coptic Christians, and the boy Anthony was carefully nurtured in that faith. When he was only twenty, his parents died, leaving their land and wealth to him. One day in church he heard the priest read Christ's command to the rich young ruler: "One thing thou lackest; go, sell all, and give to the poor." He felt that the word was addressed to him, and he obeyed. Leaving behind all his possessions, he began the hermit life in desert solitude, which was to continue for about eighty years, with only a few interruptions. Anthony lived to be more than 100 years old. By that time, thousands upon thousands had followed his example. He himself had been the counselor of bishops and emperors. His friend, the great Athanasius, wrote his biography. It was soon translated and brought to the West where, in the strange ways of divine grace, it became an important link in the conversion of St. Augustine.

From the narrative in *The Confessions* it is clear that it was Anthony's willingness to forsake everything in his quest for life with God that made such a revolutionary impact upon Augustine. And as we read about the men and women of the desert, it is the same startling fact that stands out: they were convinced that communion with God is a priceless treasure. It was this communion, above all, that solitude gave them. Outward deprivation and discipline were but a means to that end. Life with God was the pearl of great price; to possess it they gladly sold their all.

Waddell observes how difficult it is for us today to recognize the claims of these spiritual ventures that summon all our reserves of strength and endurance in a solitary quest for the eternal one. We readily grant, she says, that the dedicated soldier, the Arctic explorer, the artist in the South Seas, the pioneer in space research, shall endure unmeasured self-denial, shall risk everything—even life itself— for their own satisfaction or for the enrichment of humankind. Only God is not deemed worthy of such sacrifice!

The dispelling of this error is the major message that sounds from the hermits of the desert. It clearly rings in the beautiful words of Paulinus of Nola, a French nobleman and ex-senator who had himself renounced worldly success to become a humble priest:

> The shows and forms of things, . . .
>   despising the loveliness
> Soliciting for ill our mortal eyes.
> The present's nothing: but eternity
> Abides for those on whom all truth, all good,
> Hath shone in some entire and perfect light.[1]

Sustained and guided by that light, the men and women of the desert gladly faced the terrors both of the life and the last enemy, death. The writings that Waddell has gathered give many pictures of the stern, rugged settings in which the monks lived out their lifelong quest. A typical passage from *The Desert Fathers* takes us to Scete, one of the most isolated but most famed centers of monastic life:

> The place in which the Holy Macarius lived was called Scete. It is set in a vast desert, a day and a night journey from the monasteries on Nitria, and the way to it is to be found or shown by no track . . . but one journeys by the signs and courses of the stars. Water is hard to find. . . . Here therefore are men made perfect in holiness; . . . yet their chief concern is the love which they show to one another and towards such as by chance reach that spot.[2]

This paragraph strikes a revealing note, very important for understanding the hermit's manner of life; the scene is desolate and harsh, but within it the fires of fraternal love glow brightly. Numerous references bear witness to this important fact. One writer gives us this vignette of brotherhood in action:

> They dwell dispersed throughout the desert and separate in their cells, but bound together by love. . . . Quiet are they and gentle. . . . They have indeed a great rivalry among them . . . . It is who shall be more merciful than his brother, kinder, humbler, more patient.[3]

Ironically, we hear most often of the extremists among the hermits— such as Simeon Stylites spending many years atop his pillar. But these were the rare exceptions. Most of the desert-dwellers were earnest people of God, even though their concept of following Christ lacked a vision of the world-affirming and world-serving qualities proclaimed in the New Testament. They saw only "in a mirror dimly" the meaning of freedom in Christ, but their passionate purpose to follow the will of God cannot be questioned. Says Abbot Abraham,

> We are not ignorant that in our land there are fair and secret places where there be fruit trees in plenty . . . and the richness of the land would give us our daily bread with very little bodily toil. . . . But we have despised all these and with them all the luxurious pleasures of the world: we have joy in this desolation, and to all delight do we prefer the dread vastness of this solitude.[4]

For thousands of people, this stern choice became the gateway to a life of prayer and self-giving love to both God and humanity. John Cassian, a notable fifth-century writer who had spent some years among the hermits in Egypt and to whom we owe so much of our knowledge of the desert fathers, gives us this picture of the "reward unspeakable" that came to some of those who braved the path of desolation in quest of the greatest riches of all—the moment of mystic vision when

> beyond sound of voice or movement of the tongue or any uttered word, when the mind is narrowed by no human speech, but . . . all its senses gathered in one round, leaps like a fountain toward God, discovering in one brief particle of time such things as cannot easily be spoken, . . . when all love, all longing, all desire, all seeking, all thoughts of ours, all that we see, all that we say, all that we hope, shall be God.[5]

The Desert Fathers is a series of kaleidoscopic pictures of human life reduced to rest utter simplicity as far as "daily bread" is concerned, but ever richly provided with the break of the soul. Perhaps few of us will read the entire book, and so succeed in envisioning all the changing scenes. But even gleaning scattered portions will yield a rich harvest for the contemporary Christian.

Among the treasures brought to us in these writings are the tales, many very strange and some no doubt apocryphal, of moving spiritual experience—of Paul the First Hermit, deep in the desert, saintly and humble, visited by St. Anthony as he neared death in his 113th year, buried with the assistance of friendly lions; of the holy Paphnutius, who by his humility and his keen understanding of humanity was able to lead people of many different callings to God; of Abbot Abraham, who donned other garments and went without fear into the bedroom of a brother to win his niece back to Christ; of the blessed Pambo, who "made so light of silver and gold that verily he seemed to have fulfilled the Lord's commandment"; and the Lady Melania, whom Pambo taught that generosity is truest when concealed. The presence and work of the Holy Spirit stand clearly revealed in stories such as these and many others similar to them.

The "Sayings of the Fathers" make up a major part of Waddell's book. Here the wisdom of the monks is distilled in brief paragraphs, or even single sentences, revealing a great depth of spiritual understanding, and frequently, too, a profound psychological insight into the motives, the moral struggles, and the sins of people. For monks remain human. Statements like those below are as valid today as in the fifth century.

The abbot Antony said, "Who sits in solitude and is quiet hath escaped from three wars: hearing, speaking, seeing; yet against one thing shall he continually battle: that is, his own heart."[6]

The abbess Matrona said, . . . "It is better to have many about thee, and to live the solitary life in thy will, than to be alone and the desire of thy mind be with the crowd."[7]

The abbot Macarius said, "If in desiring to rebuke any one thou art thyself moved to anger, thou dost satisfy thine own passion; in saving another, lose not thyself."[8]

The holy Syncletica said, "A treasure that is known is quickly spent; and even so any virtue that is commented on and made a public show of is destroyed. Even as wax is melted before the face of fire, so is the soul enfeebled by praise, and loses the toughness of its virtues."[9]

A certain brother had sinned, and the priest commanded him to go out from the church. But Bessarion rose up and went out with him, saying, "I, too, am a sinful man."[10]

An old man said, "See that thou despise not the brother that stands by thee; for thou knowest not whether the spirit of God be in thee or in him."[11]

As he lay dying, Paphnutius said, "No one in this world ought to be despised, let him be a thief, or an actor on the stage, or one that tilled the ground . . . for in every condition of human life there are souls that please God and have their hidden deeds wherein he takes delight."[12]

The abbot Mathois said, "The nearer a man approaches to God, the greater sinner he sees himself to be."[13]

In addition to the moving tales and the capsulized wisdom, a third important element in these writings is the many memorable characters to whom they introduce us. We can mention only a few:

There is Macarius the Good. One of the stories told about him is that he came to his hut one day to find someone thieving there. Macarius stood by like an obliging stranger, and then helped the intruder load his animal, and finally led him out, making no noise. "But Macarius," the brethren said, "was like God, who shields the world and bears its sin."[14]

There is Bishop Nonnus of Edessa, attending a bishops' meeting in Antioch. During their gathering Pelagia the courtesan rode by, dressed in jewels and splendor. While the other bishops turned their eyes away, Nonnus freely continued to look at Pelagia, both because he admired her beauty and because her care for her outward appearance put to shame his comparative negligence in caring for his soul. And not many days later, we are told, the bishop's preaching won Pelagia's heart for Christ.

There is Benus, of whom the brethren declared "that never had an oath or lie come from his mouth, nor had any of mankind ever seem him angry, or saying an unnecessary or idle word, but that his life went by in a great silence, . . . and in all things he lived as an angel might: moreover he was of vast humility . . . and did reckon himself of no account."[15]

Beneath the stories, the words, and the lives of the desert fathers lay the deeper reality that they ever saw and sought to communicate: the *eternal setting*, which is the true environment of the human. It is this setting—the soul alone before its maker and judge—that it is so hard for contemporary men and women to discern and experience. The desert ideal, "to be alone with the Alone," eludes us. We become great, and God becomes small. But this was not so for the desert fathers. As Waddell says,

> They thought to devaluate time by setting it over against eternity, and instead they have given it an unplumbed depth. . . . The sense of infinity is now in our blood.[16]

> Their every action shows a standard of values that turns the world upside-down. It was their humility, their gentleness, their heart-breaking courtesy that was the seal of their sanctity, . . . far beyond abstinence or miracle or sign.[17]

From other writers we may learn and be gripped by other values—the joys of social fellowship, appreciation of the beauty of nature, the blessings of the Christian family, the meaning of human history, the intricate wonders of the created world. From the desert fathers we learn, as from scarcely any other spiritual ancestors, the riches of being alone with God.

3

The Little Flowers
of St. Francis

Anonymous

*Wherefore he chose to live rather for all men than for
his single self, inspired by the example of Him
Who brooked to die, One Man for all.*

More than 700 years intervened between the death of St. Augustine
and the birth of Francis of Assisi, whose life enkindled the most far-flung
spiritual awakening that came to Christendom in the Middle Ages.
Francis has often been called the greatest follower of Christ after
St. Paul. Whether so or not, it is certain that the life and spirit of
"the little poor man of Assisi" have had a universality of appeal and an
influence that is difficult to overstate. The story of how the voice of God
came to him, summoning him to his life work, is told in simple words in
The Life by St. Bonaventura:

On a certain day, when he had gone forth to meditate in the fields, he was walking nigh the church of St. Damian, . . . and, at the prompting of the Spirit, went within to pray. . . . As with eyes full of tears he gazed upon the Lord's cross, he heard with his bodily ears a voice proceeding from that cross, saying thrice, "Francis, go and repair My House, which, as thou seest, is falling utterly into ruin." Francis trembled. . . . When at last he came unto himself again, he prepared to obey.[1]

The whole church, through all subsequent centuries, was to feel the effects of St. Francis's obedience. Francis was born in 1182, the son of a wealthy cloth merchant, Pietro di Bernadone. As a youth he was gentle, but also zestful, fun-loving, and full of energy. He quickly won friends, both by his attractive personality and by his spendthrift generosity. Though never involved in the dangerous vices or addictions, he became known throughout the city as a leader of youth in revelry and folly. When Francis was about twenty years old, Assisi went to war with a neighboring city. Francis was captured in battle and spent a frustrating year in prison.

This experience, and a long period of illness that followed, led to his awakening to more serious thoughts about the meaning of life. Restless and dissatisfied, he began to search for God. The events connected with his conversion, culminating in his hearing the voice of Christ in St. Damian's call to service, came when he was about twenty-five years old. Taking this call seriously, he sold all his possessions and gave the money to help repair the little church. But he could already see that a more far-reaching task awaited him. As the voice of Christ had said to him, the church was falling into ruin and was in deep need of renewal. The reign of Innocent III, pope at the time of Francis's conversion, is commonly called the high point of papal power. But beneath the outward splendor lay widespread corruption and utter worldliness.

Francis soon became the friend and companion of the poor and the outcast. He took a special interest in the lepers, washing their sores. One day in a dramatic gesture in the public square of Assisi, he announced that he was taking "Lady Poverty" as his bride. His father was furious when he learned that Francis had been giving away all his money, and, hauling him before the bishop, threatened to deprive him of his whole inheritance. But Francis was unmoved. He renounced his father, giving his rich clothing back to him and saying,

Hitherto I have called thee my father on earth, but henceforth I can confidently say, "Our Father Which art in heaven" with Whom I have laid up my whole treasure.[2]

With a transfigured heart and a strange revolutionary spirit, he began challenging the ways of both the church and the world of his time, seeking to follow the example of Jesus in poverty, humility, and love for other people. What he himself practiced, he began to teach to a growing circle of followers who gathered around him. His program, as he lived and taught it, is summarized in a sermon he preached at a chapter meeting some years later. In this sermon, he encouraged the friars

to reverence and obedience to Holy Mother Church, and to sweet brotherly love, to pray for all the people of God, to have patience in the adversities of the world and temperance in prosperity, to maintain an angelic purity and chastity, to remain at peace and harmony with God and with men and with their own conscience, to humility and meekness toward all, to the contempt of the world and a love and fervent practice of holy poverty.[3]

Francis had been called to "repair the church," but he was to accomplish this not by an outward revolution. Rather, his aim and program were to rebuild from within. Only then could there be a real and enduring renewal in the house of God.

Stories about St. Francis began to be written down not long after his death, and many were soon published as biographies. *The Little Flowers* was written considerably later, first in a Latin text by Brother Ugolino, and then fifty years later in Italian by a gifted but anonymous author. Although it is most popular of all books about St. Francis, *The Little Flowers* is not a biography, nor even altogether reliable history. Rather it is a supplement, embellished from the loving memories of his followers, to the earlier biographies issued about 150 years after the death of St. Francis. But its essential message is so moving and convincing that even the tales that are clearly fictionalized bring us vividly into the presence of the Christlike spirit of the saint.

Early in his ministry, says the beautiful *Little Flowers* story, Francis "was placed in a great agony of doubt" as to whether he should engage in a public ministry or spend his time in a ministry devoted to prayer.

Anxious to know the will of God in the matter, he did not trust just his own judgment. He sent one of his companions to ask in prayer for guidance by two of his closest spiritual friends. Both of them received from Christ the same clear answer: "He wants you to go about the world preaching, because God did not call you for yourself alone, but also for the salvation of others."[4] Francis accepted this answer with great gladness, and set forth at once with two companions, "all aflame with divine power."

Such a spirit, embodying and revealing the love of Christ, could not fail to be a powerful influence on those who came into touch with him. Both his example and his words were filled with transforming power. Having enjoyed the hospitality of a nobleman and been treated with unusual courtesy, he interpreted this kindness as a signal to bring the nobleman to the service of Christ.

Clara Favorino, a gifted young noblewoman of Assisi, was inspired by the lifestyle and responded to its challenge. A little later, with his help, she founded the Second Order for women, and thereby "as anew a tender glory over the religious revival." Bernard, the first convert in the movement, was won through observing Francis's devoted example and prayer life. Silvester, an avaricious businessman drawn by the wonderful generosity Francis and Bernard showed him, gave up his wealth to the brotherhood.

A strong missionary emphasis was at the heart of Francis's program; to win people to Christ was his goal and his joy. Shortly after the order had gained approval in Rome, he set out on a mission to the Moslems during one of the Crusades. This effort did not succeed, but passing unharmed through the battle lines, Francis did have an opportunity to preach before the Sultan,who heard his message with deep respect.

In obedience to the answer given to the intercession by his friends, Francis divided his time between the inner life of prayer and the outward life of soul-winning. While reading *The Little Flowers*, one hardly knows which to admire more: the beauty of Francis's own life in Christ or the transforming influence he had on his followers. Of St. Francis's own Christlike qualities, one of the most outstanding was surely his humility, so well illustrated by his seeking the guidance of God through the prayers of coworkers. Many other incidents reveal the same trait. When asked why he, rather than someone else, had been selected by God to lead the movement, he answered after a moment's thought that it was perhaps because he of all people had least to boast of in himself, and therefore God could trust him.

His humility also expressed itself in a gentle and forgiving spirit toward all humanity. For example, when one of the brothers drove away some robbers with angry words, Francis sent him out to find the robbers and ask their pardon. All three robbers were thus brought back to God.

This quality of gentleness was surely one secret of Francis's influence over animals, though no doubt there is much that is exaggerated about these strange tales. He preached to the birds, and they were quiet until he pronounced the benediction, then they flew away in good order. He took time to free some doves and make a nest for them; and while doing so won the allegiance of the young lad who had ensnared them. He calmed the fierce wolf of Gubbio so the people of the community no longer needed to be afraid. St. Francis was indeed an "instrument of peace," both in the human world and beyond. Divine grace seems to have granted him "a new adjustment to the world revealed only to the singularly pure in heart."

Many *Little Flowers* tales speak with admiration of St. Francis's ability to read the hearts and understand the characters of those with whom he dealt. He knows that Brother Rufino is among the saintliest of men, "but St. Francis never said those words in the presence of Brother Rufino."[5] He reproves Brother Elias, one of the most "difficult" of his companions, for his pride. He prophesies the suicide of Brother Giovanni, we are startled to read. But he is gentle and kind to all, good and evil. He reads the rancorous thoughts of hatred in the mind of one who has thereby admitted a devil into the fellowship, but as soon as the sin is confessed, it is forgiven.

In a village where he first preached, his message was so well received that all the people wanted to join the order; but Francis told them not to decide too quickly, and in his mind he began to plan the organization of a Third Order to be made up entirely of lay people who continued in their regular callings but still followed certain religious devotions and services "for the salvation of all People everywhere." Thieves and robbers joined the order because he dared to treat them as people.

St. Francis's public ministry was as effective as his private ministry. Here is a typical picture of his preaching at Bologna:

> When the entire square was filled with men and women and students, St. Francis stood up on a high place in the center and began to preach what the Holy Spirit dictated to him. And he preached such marvelous and astounding things that he seemed to be not a man but an angel. His heavenly words seemed like sharp arrows which were shot from the bow of divine wisdom and pierced the hearts of everyone so effectively that by this sermon he converted a very great multitude of men and women from a state of sin to remorse and penance.[6]

During the foundation days of the Order, Francis and his companions made memorable contributions to the fulfillment of the Franciscan ideal, though the influence of Francis always was clearly dominant. This is strikingly portrayed in the symbolic vision of one of the bothers, James of Massa, in which Christ calls St. Francis and gives him "a chalice full of the spirit of life" and says to him, "Go and visit your friars and let them drink from this chalice."[7]

The many varieties of Christlikeness revealed in the lives of the Little Brothers make it difficult to select any particular one for special comment. In *The Little Flowers* there seems to be a preference for telling about those whose service to the Franciscan cause was marked by special humility and self-forgetfulness. One such person was Brother John of Penna, described as "a man of great devotion and prayer" and "always a man with joy and peace of mind." At a very young age, he volunteered to go on a mission to Provence, which was then regarded as a foreign field. When he had spent twenty-five years there, he return to the home base in Italy. Reassigned to another field, he served there for an even longer period, and in the same spirit. As death approached him, however, fierce temptations no doubt assailed him—as is so often the case with God's faithful servants. But another of the inconspicuous Franciscans, Brother Matthew, was able to lead Brother John out of despair into the life of a renewed faith by pointing to God's great mercy in Christ. Then death had no terror for him.[8]

Concerning the saintly Brother Bernard, we read that when he was sent to Bologna by St. Francis to found a new work there, he was insulted and ridiculed by the children in the public square for his simple, ragged garb. When he endured this abuse with great patience and gentleness, it so impressed a judge in the city that the judge donated a furnished house to the order as a place of mission. And the judge,

The Little Flowers says, "henceforth became a father and a special protector to Brother Bernard and his companions."[9]

These are but a few of the holy companions to whom St. Francis gave "the chalice of the spirit of life." They typify thousands. And despite the storms that have swept over the order, it still lives and serves humankind, ever challenged and inspired by the spirit of its founder.

The crowning experience of St. Francis's life was his receiving the "stigmata," the marks of the crucified Christ, on his hands, feet, and side. A wealthy friend had given the order a lovely and rugged mountain, called La Verna, as a suitable retreat for solitude and meditation. After the close of a large chapter meeting in 1224, Francis retired to this mountain, proposing to make a long fast there. After some days, leaving behind the group that had accompanied him, he went into complete solitude. J. O. Dobson, a Franciscan biographer, has written of that ordeal:

> It was the final contest of this faith with evil, the complete submission of his spirit to this Lord. But he knew also that ineffable joy and illumination, when it seemed that he was indeed sharing in the Eternal Life.[10]

One day, as he was praying before his little cell, there came a vision clothed in light. "The face was gracious and beautiful beyond telling, yet it was a face of suffering."[11] When the vision had passed, Francis could see that in his own body he had received the "final seal," the marks of the Crucified.

This supreme "fellowship of the cross" was the culmination of a life of hardship, affliction, and anguish. Few religious leaders have had to bear more suffering than St. Francis of Assisi: suffering within, in a frail and disease-racked body; and suffering without, in misunderstanding, rejection, and persecution. Nevertheless the dominant note of his whole life was joy—joy in God and in all the wonders of his creation, joy in Christ the Savior and friend of sinners. A passage in one of the Franciscan chronicles tells us that one day St. Francis and Brother Giles were descending the lovely wooded hillside leading down to the Marshes of Ancona. As they walked,

> Francis sang aloud in French, praising and blessing the Lord for His goodness. For they felt their hearts overflow with fervent joy, as though they had acquired an immense treasure.[12]

They had begun their blessed new life in extreme poverty, but God was leading them into a part of the land where their work would bear bounteous fruit. And so they sang. In the lovely "Canticle of the Sun" written near the end of his life, Francis has given the most famous expression to his joy in God and in the creation. Among its beautiful stanzas are these:

> Be praised, my Lord, for Sister Water,
>> who is very useful and humble and chaste!

> Be praised, my Lord, for Brother Fire,
>> by whom you give us light at night,
>> and he is beautiful and merry and mighty and strong.

> Be praised, my Lord, for our sister Mother Earth,
>> who sustains and governs us,
>> and produces fruits with colorful flowers and leaves!

> Be praised, my Lord, for our Sister Bodily Death,
>> from whom no living man can escape.[13]

It is not strange that at the end, when hardship and illness had done their work on his frail body and one of his friends told him that death was near, "blessed Francis was seen from these words to derive a new joy to his mind." Calling Brother Angelo and Brother Leo to his side, he told them to sing to him of Sister Death. And so those two brethren sang, with many tears, the Song of Brother Sun.

Only a few days later they carried him, at his request, down to the Portiuncula, the first home of the order. There they obeyed him when he asked to be laid naked on the ground, on the breast of Sister Mother Earth, that he might breathe his last breath there. He died on October 4, 1226, at the age of forty-four, after twenty years of earnest following in the footsteps of the master whom he loved. Two years later his friend and protector, Pope Gregory IX, responded to the convictions in the hearts of tens of thousands by enrolling his name among those "whom the Church delights to honor," the calendar of saints. Perhaps concerning no other name on the list has there been more universal agreement throughout all Christendom, both then and now.

To read *The Little Flowers* is to be carried back across the centuries into the presence of this unique saint, and into the glad company of those whom his life had inspired and illuminated. Who can lay the book down and turn away without a new-kindled desire to be a better Christian?

4

The Imitation of Christ

Thomas à Kempis

All is vanity, save to love God and serve Him only.

During the fourteenth and fifteenth centuries in western Europe, especially in the Low Countries and along the Rhine, there were strong movements that sought to promote a deeper and purer Christian life among both clergy and lay people. One of these movements, called "The Brethren of the Common Life," was centered in a famous school and community at Deventer, founded by Gerhard de Groote, a gifted educator and ardent spiritual leader. De Groote, born in Deventer in 1340, came from a wealthy family and had an excellent university education. He began what promised to be a brilliant teaching career. Then at about age thirty-five, he experienced a radical conversion after which his manner of life was completely changed. For about three years he lived in a monastery. Then, upon the advice of the great spiritual teacher Jan van Ruysbroek, he accepted a commission as a missionary preacher in the diocese of Utrecht. Though never ordained, he spent several years traveling, preaching against ecclesiastical abuses and calling the people to repentance, until his stern message led to his commission being withdrawn. During those years, it is said, the people of Holland were stirred toward God as they have never otherwise been. De Groote's life and preaching were cut short, however. While bringing medical help to someone suffering from the plague, he himself was stricken and soon afterward died at the age forty-four. But his dedicated life had sown seeds that were to bear rich fruit in thousands of his followers.

Like their founder and leader, members of the Brethren of the Common Life recognized the widespread corruption that was prevalent in the church, and many of them boldly protested and preached against it. At Deventer and in their other communities, some of the brethren lived together in brotherhood houses; others continued their ordinary lives in the world. All of them had as their aim a higher level of spiritual life, including both a "closer walk with God" for themselves and more devoted service to their fellowmen. One of their most effective instruments for carrying out their program was founding and conducting Christian schools. Both in the Low Countries and in Germany, the schools of the Brethren became the most famous of their time. Albert Hyma, a distinguished historian of the movement, has given this picture of their life and activities:

> They taught and preached love, obedience, peace, and humility, fed the poor, sheltered the homeless, cured the sick, reformed monasteries, corrected abuses, and wrote books like *The Imitation*. They shared the fate of the "hidden saints," whose names seldom if ever appear in our newspapers but whose influence is often much greater than that of a heretic or a hero, or a scoundrel.[1]

The Brethren were ardent reformers, but not revolutionaries. They aimed to renew the life of the church from within. The quiet work of the Brethren of the Common Life marked, in fact, a mighty movement of the Spirit. Through their schools and through contacts among ordinary citizens, their influence spread from the Low Countries to Germany, Switzerland, France, and beyond. Many of the great scholars and church leaders of the time had been their students. Their program of spiritual renewal, called the "Devotio Moderna," led multitudes into a new life of

Christian love and freedom. And when, after a time, the movement lost its force and one by one its schools closed, the call to penitence and faith and to a consecrated walk with God lived on through the pages of the remarkable little book, *The Imitation of Christ*.

In 1392, a young German student named Thomas Haemerken (later known as Thomas à Kempis) came to Deventer. Seven years later, Thomas entered the monastery in nearby Zwolle, where he continued to live until his death in 1471 at the age of ninety-one. His life as a monk might seem to have been quite uneventful: studying, writing, copying manuscripts; but through it we have been given one of the most beloved and influential books ever written. In recent years, some scholars have held that Gerhard de Groote himself was the author of large portions of *The Imitation of Christ*, and that Thomas à Kempis was merely the compiler and copyist. Even if this should prove to be true, the book has still come to us through Thomas, with whose name it has been associated from the beginning. The exhortation found in *The Imitation* itself is relevant at this point: "As not who said this, or that, but mark what is spoken."[2]

The Imitation is made up of only four short "books." Three of these consist of brief meditations, prayers, and precepts concerning the Christian life with God. The fourth is a treatise on the Sacrament of the Altar (or Holy Communion), giving pastoral guidance as to its right reception. Written in Latin, the book has since been translated into numerous languages, appearing in an estimated 6,000 editions.

Yet even so great and so beloved a book has not been without its critics. Some have said that it preaches asceticism too strongly, making it appear that Christianity consists in giving up all the joy and pleasures of life. In answer to this, it should be pointed out that what is recommended is asceticism with a purpose. All life needs to be disciplined. Christ, too, bore much hardship and taught his followers that the way to life is narrow and often difficult. And far from presenting merely a gloomy and joyless view of life, *The Imitation* clearly points to the secret of true and abiding joy, namely a good conscience: "If the conscience be at peace, thou wilt never lack joy," says a key passage in Book II.[3]

Another common criticism of *The Imitation* is that its emphasis is too individualistic: we are to "work out our own salvation," but with too little concern about the social aspects of religion. These objections may have a certain validity, but no book can serve every need. *The Imitation* was not designed as a book of prayers, but rather as a guide for the individual pilgrim. It teaches that prayers and devotion are good in themselves, entirely apart from any social purpose they may serve. And its presupposition is that the individual's sincere walk with God will inevitably also nourish the roots of social good and true Christian community. It has been well pointed out that nothing in *The Imitation* would reveal the interest of the Brethren of the Common Life in education, yet their schools flourished throughout western Europe.

To offset such criticism, we have the testimony of thousands that here is indeed a book that can minister to the needs of the human heart. Throughout the whole world, people have been nourished and inspired by its wisdom, Ignatius Loyola, the founder of the Jesuits, always kept it on the table in his room. Dag Hammarskjöld, former secretary general of the United Nations, made it his constant companion. Spiritual teacher Douglas Steere said although he at first a reluctant reader of the book, he came to treasure its message.

The reasons for such a universal appeal are not too hard to discern when we begin to examine more closely the basic teachings of *The Imitation*. Far from being merely negative and repressive, it sets forth in chiselled perspective the great positive principles of Christian living. Its words are often deceptively simple. But they challenge the soul in its depths. In the first three books of *The Imitation* we find constant emphasis upon such central and basic principles of Christian practice as those listed below:

1. Prayer: There is no greater good than prayer. It is of the very essence of the Kingdom of God. "Learn to despise all outward things, devoting thyself to spiritual things only, and thou wilt perceive the Kingdom of God come unto thee."[4] "Christ will come unto thee, and give thee His consolation, if thou prepare for Him in thy heart a worthy dwelling place."[5] This inward communion with God is the heart of the prayer life. "The inward man He often visiteth, sweetly communing with him, and granting unto him gracious comfort, peace, and wonderful friendship."[6] The whole *Imitation* is a guide to just such a deep prayer life. Many of its most moving passages are in fact prayers, in which the needs of the individual are laid open before God for his help and healing.

2. *Reading the Scriptures:* The Bible should be read with faith and devotion. Mere argument about the Scriptures or too much attention to "curiosity of style" can deprive us of deeper values. "If thou desire to reap benefit [by reading of the Scriptures], read with humility, simplicity, and faith; nor ever crave the reputation of learning."[7]

3. *Surrender of the will to God:* God has given us our will, in order that we may yield it up and thereby find true freedom. And if we ask, "How often shall I resign myself" and "Wherein shall I forsake myself?" the answer is uncompromising:

> Always yea, every hour; in small things and in great. Thou must divest thyself of self in all things. For how canst thou be Mine and I thine, unless, both inwardly and outwardly, thou be stripped of all self-will? . . . Forsake thyself, resign thyself, and thou wilt enjoy great inward peace, Give all for all: ask for nothing; require nothing back; abide purely and unhesitatingly in Me, and thou wilt possess Me. Then shalt thou be free in heart, and no darkness shall burden thy spirit.[8]

Chapter 37 of Book III is one of the finest statements of the Christian's secret to a happy life that has ever been written. In few places does God's call to us sound more clearly, more lovingly, and more convincingly.

4. *Self-discipline:* To live the Christian life is a lifelong task. We must learn to live with others, with ourselves, and with God. And this all requires discipline. We need to know ourselves and especially our weaknesses. "We frequently do evil, and, what is worse, we excuse it. Oftentimes we are moved with passion and think it to be zeal."[9] Even our concern for others' spiritual welfare must be disciplined: "If one that hath been once or twice admonished will not yield, contend not with him, but commit all to God, that His will may be done."[10]

One of the most important forms of self-discipline is the frequent withdrawal from others in order to seek inward quiet. Most of us talk too much, and thereby our "spiritual strength oozes away." "Only he that loveth seclusion may safely appear abroad without fear of hurt to his soul."[11]

5. Humility: Christ was meek in heart. To follow him may at times be difficult for our ego. "It is oftentimes profitable to us that other men know and reprove our faults, for thus only do we preserve our humility."[12] To hear others praised while we ourselves are overlooked is difficult but salutary. To be opposed and misunderstood when we know we are in the right is likewise hard but healthy. The standards of humility set by *The Imitation* are high: "Think not that thou hast made any progress in the things of the spirit unless thou esteem thyself inferior to all men."[13]

6. The guidance of the Spirit: For the author of *The Imitation*, the possibility of clear inner direction by the Holy Spirit was very real. He says,

> Moses hesitated not at all times to have recourse to the Tabernacle when beset by doubts and dangers, resorting to prayer for God's help and guidance against the iniquities of men. So oughtest thou in like manner, to take refuge within the secret chamber of thine heart, beseeching earnestly the divine favor.[14]

Without the inward illumination of the Spirit, even the sacred words of Scripture are not a sufficient guide. So he prays earnestly for "the word and light from above":

> Let not Moses, nor any of the Prophets, speak to me; but do Thou speak unto me, O Lord God, Who dost inspire and enlighten all the prophets. Thou alone without their aid, canst perfectly instruct me. . . . They speak most beautifully, but if Thou be silent, they inflame not the heart. They give the letter, but Thou only canst enlighten the understanding.[15]

7. Love: The greatest of Christian virtues is love. In *The Imitation* it is praised and enjoyed again and again. The great "Hymn of Love" in Book III, chapter 5, is worthy of being compared with Paul's hymn in 1 Corinthians 13, as a few excerpts here indicate:

> Love is a great thing, yea, great and good beyond comprehension; love alone lighteneth every burden, and maketh the rough places smooth. For the burden it carrieth becometh like unto no burden, and everything that is bitter it maketh sweet and wholesome. . . . Nothing is sweeter than

love: nothing stronger, nothing higher, nothing is wider, nothing more pleasant, nothing fuller or better in Heaven or earth; for love is born of God and can not rest save in God, above all created things. . . .

Let me sing the song of love; let me follow Thee, my Beloved into High Heaven, and let my soul consume herself in praising Thee, rejoicing for love. Let me love Thee more than myself, and myself only for Thee.[16]

8. *Practical judgment*: The Christian life is not an unattainable ideal. It sets high but not impossible goals. It recognizes that our lives must be lived in the midst of earth's limitations. *The Imitation* again and again points out the need for sound practical judgment in dealing with our problems. When we weary of spiritual activities and lose taste for prayer and meditation, we are told it is often a good thing to turn to bodily work for change and refreshment. Such activity, too, is the work of God. In due season the hunger for spiritual activities will return. Repeated spiritual renewal is both a possibility and a necessity all through life:

All is not lost, although thou dost oftentimes feel thyself troubled or grievously tempted. Thou art a man, and not God; thou art flesh and not an angel. How canst thou hope to abide always in the same state of virtue, when even an angel in Heaven, and the first man in paradise, did fall? I am He that raiseth up to safety then . . . that are conscious of their own infirmity.[17]

9. *Cross-bearing:* Life for the Christian is never a path of roses; rather, it frequently involves wearing a crown of thorns. "Jesus now hath many lovers of His Heavenly kingdom, but few bearers of his Cross; He hath many that are desirous of consolation, but few of tribulation."[18] Christ himself deliberately chose the way of the cross as the fundamental pattern of his life. "He that bore His own cross is gone before and showeth thee the way. he died for thee upon the Cross, that thou also shouldst bear thy cross, and for Love of Him, be ready to die on the Cross."[19] If there had been any better way for the health of person's spiritual life than to suffer, our Lord Jesus would have showed it by word and by example. Yet even the heaviest cross leads at last to liberation and to joy. "If thou bear the Cross willingly, it will bear thee, and lead thee to the end thou desirest."[20]

After the strenuous teachings of the first three books of *The Imitation*, Book IV is a heart-searching commentary on the chief source of needed strength: the Sacrament of Holy Communion. The Sacrament is a wonderful gift of God to his children—the gift of himself to unworthy sinners:

> Thou, O Lord, my God, True God and man art wholly contained in a little likeness of Bread and Wine.[21]

> Rejoice, o my soul, and give thanks unto God for so noble a gift and so precious a comfort.[22]

We cannot really understand the sacrament, says *The Imitation*. We can only come, to receive it in humility and reverence, to experience its value and power.

In the sacrament, God gives himself to us. But an important part of the Holy Communion is also the offering of ourselves to him. We give him all our sin and transgression, to be forgiven and cleansed away. We give him all our good deeds, though they are few and imperfect, that he may sanctify them. We offer him the intercessions of all who love us and have asked us to pray for them. We offer our prayers for all who have offended us in any way, and for all those against whom we have sinned in any way, that God may forgive us all together, and remove whatever is evil from our hearts.

To receive the sacrament worthily, we must be rightly prepared. "For every one that loveth prepareth for his beloved the best and fairest place, for thus he showeth the measure of his affection."[23] We must repent and turn away from every sin. Yet, we cannot do this by ourselves. Only his grace can make us ready, "as if a beggar were invited to sup with a rich man, and could make no return other than that of humble thanks and gratitude."[24]

With such an attitude we are not even to try to understand the mystery of the sacrament, but simply receive it with a humble trusting heart:

> Go forward, therefore, with simple and undoubting faith, and with the reverence of a suppliant, draw near to the Holy Sacrament; and whatsoever thou art not able to understand, commit securely to Almighty God.

God deceiveth thee not: he is deceived that trusteth too much on himself. God walketh with the simple, revealeth Himself to the humble, giveth understanding to the little ones. . . .

All reason and nature search out to follow Faith, not to go before it, nor to break in upon it.[25]

The teaching of the whole *Imitation* is basic, unadorned, and penetrating to the very heart of our spiritual situation and need. For centuries now its wise counsel has helped to answer the prayer with which Book III closes: "Defend and keep my soul amidst so many perils of the corruptible life, and, Thy grace going with me, guide me in the way of peace to the land of everlasting light."[26] Many of the briefer statements of *The Imitation* are as familiar as the words of the Bible, and as filled with proverbial wisdom. Gems such as these occur on nearly every page:

There is no true liberty save in the fear of God and a good conscience.[27]

Men pass away; but the truth of the Lord remaineth forever.[28]

I had rather feel contrition than understand the definition thereof.[29]

An humble rustic that serveth God is better than a proud philosopher who, neglecting the good life, contemplateth the courses of the stars.[30]

True peace of heart is to be had not by giving way to, but by resisting the passions.[31]

Man weigheth thine actions, but God weigheth thine intentions.[32]

It is good that at times we are called upon to bear adversities and crosses, for these oftentimes induce a man to re-enter his own heart.[33]

Gather some profit to thy soul wheresoever thou may be.[34]

He doeth most that loveth much.[35]

Is a man ever the better for being esteemed great of men?[36]

We may readily admit that if we were limited to *The Imitation* alone, it would not be a fully adequate guide for life. Undoubtedly it does not set forth clearly enough how we come to Christ, though it gives profound guidance as to how we are to follow him. Furthermore, Thomas à Kempis wrote as a monk for monks, and some of his statements do not apply outside the monastery. But knowing these limitations, no thoughtful reader can escape the force of *The Imitation*'s key teachings. The essence of the life in Christ is pointedly delineated over and over again: the full surrender of ourselves to God, a keen obedience to conscience, the reverent study of the Scriptures, the cultivation of humility and brotherly love toward all people, the necessity of cross-bearing and of a deep and continuous life of prayer. Through *The Imitation of Christ*, Gerhard de Groote and the Brethren of the Common Life have for more than 500 years become the teachers of the whole Christian world. Outside the Bible, it is probably the world's most read Christian book.

5

The Freedom of the Christian

Martin Luther

*As our heavenly Father has in Christ freely come to our aid, we
also ought freely to help our neighbor, . . . and each one
should become as it were a Christ to the other . . .
that we may be truly Christians.*

"Out of the strong came something sweet," says an Old Testament
riddle based on Samson's experience of finding honey in the body of a
dead lion. Power and peaceableness are not incompatible; both are
common characteristics of God's great followers. Thus David, a man of
war, also wrote the beautiful Twenty-third Psalm about green pastures
and still waters. Our Lord, whose threatening words of rebuke drove the
traffickers from the temple, also gently took little children in his arms
and blessed them. Martin Luther, whose life marked the transition to the
modern period of church history, was a man of war in the spiritual

sphere. His adult life was filled with controversy and struggle for the purification and renewal of the church. Luther's spirit and his fearlessness in the face of enemies are mirrored in the lines of his great reformation hymn:

> And though this world, with devils filled,
> Should threaten to undo us;
> We will not fear, for God hath willed
> His truth to triumph through us.

Yet it was this same Martin Luther who in the year 1520, in the midst of his conflict with the papacy, wrote the beautiful devotional tract *The Freedom of the Christian* (or *Christian Liberty*). There he set forth, with simplicity and clarity, the essence of Christian faith and life. True, even this treatise is not without its controversial elements, but this is minimal; the basic argument is concerned with the person's life with God, what it is, how it is achieved, and how it expresses itself in outward life and conduct. The book is dedicated to Pope Leo X, whom Luther calls "a lamb in the midst of wolves" and "a Daniel among lions" because of the evil forces that surrounded the pope. And although Luther wrote in a humble spirit, he was well aware that he had produced a truly great piece of writing. In his letter to the Pope he says,

> It is a small book if you regard its size. Unless I am mistaken, however, it contains the whole of Christian life in a brief form, provided you grasp its meaning. I am a poor man and have no other gift to offer, and you do not need to be enriched by any but a spiritual gift.[1]

The judgment of subsequent generations has confirmed Luther's evaluation of the work. Martin Luther, the son of a miner, was born in 1483 in Eisleben, Germany. The outward course of his life is readily charted by dates and events of significance: his entering the Augustinian monastery at Erfurt in 1505; his appointment as professor of theology at the University of Wittenberg in 1508; his nailing the Ninety-five Theses to the door of the Castle Church in 1517; his historic trial and defense at Worms in 1521; his translation of the New Testament into German in 1522 (and the whole Bible in 1534); his marriage to Katherina von Bora, a former nun, in 1526; writing the *Augsburg Confession* (the chief

Lutheran creedal statement) in 1530; and his death at Eisleben in 1546.

But the truly great event in Luther's life, an event for which it is difficult to give an exact date, was his breakthrough into personal faith and freedom in Christ. We know that this came to him through his study and teaching of the Scriptures; we know that it came after many years of struggling to find peace with God through his own efforts, prayers, mortifications; we know that he was greatly helped in his quest by the words of his "spiritual father," Johannes von Staupitz, the head of the monastery. But at just what moment or in what situation Luther found abiding peace, scholars are not in agreement. The important thing is that he did find the way; the light did dawn; wonderful liberation in and through the Word of God did come to him. It is of this that he writes, so earnestly and so fervently, to Pope Leo in *The Freedom of the Christian*.

Luther begins by summarizing the main argument of his treatise in a double statement, now familiar and often quoted: "A Christian is a perfectly free lord of all, and subject to none. A Christian is a perfectly dutiful servant of all, and subject to all."[2] This statement indicates the two main parts of the treatise. In the first, Luther shows how the inner person is set free by faith alone. In the second, he shows that, nevertheless, works are a necessary part of our outward existence. We live by faith, but faith necessarily issues in Christian works. A true Christian life must include both. Says Luther,

> Man has a twofold nature, a spiritual and a bodily one. According to the spiritual nature, which men refer to as the soul, he is called a spiritual, inner, or new man. According to the bodily nature, which men refer to as the flesh, he is called a carnal, outward or old man. . . . Because of this diversity of nature the Scriptures assert contradictory things concerning the same man, since these two men in the same man contradict each other.[3]

The inner person, Luther says, cannot be profited or helped by outward acts, such as eating and drinking, wearing sacred vestments in holy places, going on pilgrimages, fasting, and similar activities: "Such works produce nothing but hypocrites."[4] What the person really needs, and the only thing that it needs absolutely, is the Word of God—that is, the gospel concerning Christ, incarnate, suffering, risen, and glorified. Only by receiving this gospel can anyone be saved; and true preaching sets forth this gospel in such a way that men and women may take hold of it in faith. "One believes with the heart and so is justified" (Romans 10:10) and by no outward labor of any kind can the inward person be justified, made free, and saved.

The Scriptures are made up of precepts and promises, law and gospel. The precepts teach what is good and what ought to be done, but they give no power to do it. It is when the law has convicted people of their wrongdoing and humbled them that the gospel, the promises of God, granted by faith can set them free:

> That which is impossible for you to accomplish by trying to fulfill all the works of the law—many and useless as they all are—you will accomplish quickly and easily through faith. God our Father has made all things depend on faith so that whoever has faith will have everything, and whoever does not have faith will have nothing. . . . If a touch of Christ healed, how much more will this tender spiritual touch, this absorbing of the Word, communicate to the soul all things that belong to the Word. This, then, is how through faith alone without works the soul is justified by the Word of God, sanctified, made true, peaceful, and free, filled with every blessing and truly made a child of God.[5]

According to Luther, faith has such great power for three reasons: *First*, faith is in the inner person. It is not merely an external activity that may not reach the heart of people at all. Just as iron exposed to fire glows because of the fire, so the believing person is made to "flow" with life because of the indwelling Word. *Second*, faith alone truly honors God; in fact, it gives God the highest honor possible, because it holds God to be truthful and worthy of trust. What higher credit can we attribute to anyone than truth and absolute goodness? Thus the soul cleaves to the promises of God, deeming God absolutely trustworthy. *Third*, faith unites the soul to Christ, by which mystery, as the apostle Paul teaches, Christ and the soul are made "one flesh." Human marriages are but feeble types of this one great marriage:

> Christ is full of grace, life, and salvation; the soul is full of sin, death, and damnation. Now let faith come between them, and sin, death, and damnation will be Christ's, while grace, life, and salvation will be the soul's.

All this takes place, says Luther, through "the wedding ring of faith":

> Who can comprehend the riches of the glory of this grace? Here the rich
> and divine bridegroom Christ marries this poor, wicked harlot, redeems
> her from all her evil and adorns her with all his goodness!"[6]

Through faith alone we too become "priests" to God. All things are
subject to God, who both intercedes for us and teaches us inwardly
through the Spirit. And these great privileges God communicates also to
every believer: all men and women who believed in Christ are priests in
him. The believer is exalted above all things in spiritual power, so that all
are subject to him or her—for "strength is made perfect in weakness"—
and the believer can turn all things toward salvation. And we are called
to appear before God and pray for others and to teach one another mutu-
ally things that are of God. This status does not belong to a few selected
individuals, but to *all* believers—even though all are not called to teach
or preach publicly.

Those who are called to preach, however, must truly preach Christ,
that is, not only preach about Christ in a historical manner, but proclaim
him in such a way that faith is created in the hearts of the listeners so
"that He may not only be Christ but a Christ for you and for me. . . . Such
faith is produced and preserved in us by preaching why Christ came,
what he brought and bestowed, what benefit it is to us to accept Him."[7]
To be a preacher of the gospel is indeed a high, sometimes almost an
overwhelming, calling.

In his discussion of the outward self, Luther is emphatic that he does
not underrate the value of good works. Good works are an essential and
important part of the Christian life, even though they can contribute
nothing to our salvation. We are saved by faith alone—to repeat Luther's
analogy, by being "married to Christ." But when we have been saved by
faith, good works are a natural and inevitable consequence. Good works
serve especially two important purposes: first, to discipline the body,
because we are still living in a world with temptations and enticements;
and second, to serve our neighbor, who is also in this world.

Good works can never justify us before God. But our good works can
show our gratitude to God. Good works are done gratuitously. And
therefore we can also be truly effective in behalf of our neighbor. As
Christians we live not for ourselves but for others. And we do this

freely—"in the freest servitude." Thus we also follow the example of Christ, our Lord. Christ gave of himself to help others, and took the form of a servant. So should we also do for others:

> Although the Christian is thus free from all works, he ought in this liberty to empty himself, take upon himself the form of a servant, be made in the likeness of men, . . . serve, help, and in every way deal with his neighbor as he sees that God through Christ has dealt and still deals with him.[8]

Regarding the Christian's works, Luther goes on to say,

> I will therefore give myself as a Christ to my neighbor, just as Christ offered himself to me; I will do nothing in this life except what I see is necessary, profitable, and salutary to my neighbor, since through faith I have an abundance of all good things in Christ.[9]

> The good things we have from God should flow from one to the other and be common to all, so that every one should "put on" his neighbor and so conduct himself toward him as if he himself were in the other's place. . . . I should lay before God my faith and my righteousness that they may cover and intercede for the sins of my neighbor which I take upon myself and so labor and serve in them as if they were my very own. That is what Christ did for us. . . .

> We conclude, therefore, that a Christian lives not in himself, but in Christ and in his neighbor. Otherwise he is not a Christian. He lives in Christ through faith, in his neighbor through love. By faith he is caught up beyond himself into God. By love he descends beneath himself into his neighbor. Yet he always remains in God and in his love.[10]

The end of Christian faith is not only the salvation of the individual, but rather the building of true Christian community. Luther had a great vision of the kingdom—the city of the living God coming down from God out of heaven. Because of the way the gospel had been misrepresented, he seemed at times to be condemning good works of kingdom building. But this concern was simply to put the gospel as proclaimed in the New Testament into crystal-clear perspective. In *The Freedom of the*

Christian, he outlines the basics for a truly spiritual devotional life: a living faith constantly flowering forth in Christlike loving service and building the communion of saints. To see this vision of faith and works, gospel and law, in true perspective, is indeed to know the reality of Christian freedom.

6

The Interior Castle

St. Teresa of Avila

*When the silkworm is full-grown, it starts to spin its silk
and to build the house in which it is to die.*

The sixteenth century was in many respects the greatest century in the history of Spain. It was the age of exploration and swiftly expanding national power. The foundations were laid for Spanish rule in the New World; and in Europe, Spain challenged the might of England reaching toward its height under Elizabeth I. It was also the golden age of Spanish literature, the time of Cervantes and Lope de Vega. But, equally important with political and literary advances, sixteenth century Spain was marked by a remarkable flowering of the spiritual life, expressing itself in saintly lives, in a stream of notable spiritual books, and in vigorous reform movements in the church. Many of the greatest names in Spanish spirituality were from this period, including St. Teresa of Avila, John of the Cross, Luis of Granada, and Ignatius Loyola. Among them, the name St. Teresa shines most brightly of all, not only because of the profundity of her thought but also because of her message. While truly spiritual, *The Interior Castle* is geared to the level of the common reader. In the words of St. Teresa, Spanish religious writing comes to us in its most attractive and beloved form.

As St. Teresa begins *The Interior Castle*, she tells how the idea for the book came to her in answer to prayer: the idea was to picture the human soul as a beautiful castle with many rooms, and to describe the methods whereby the soul "enters into itself" in its quest for a deepening life of fellowship with God:

> While I was beseeching the Lord today that He would speak through me . . . I began to think of the soul as if it were a castle made of a single diamond or of very clear crystal, in which there are many rooms, just as in heaven there are many mansions.[1]

A little further on she continues by saying,

> Now let us return to our beautiful and delightful castle and see how we can enter it. I seem rather to be talking nonsense. . . . For we ourselves are the castle, and it would be absurd to tell someone to enter a room where he was in it already! But you must understand that there are many ways of "being" in a place. Many souls remain in the outer court of the castle, . . . and have no idea what there is in that wonderful place, or who dwells in it, or even how many rooms it has. You will have read certain books on prayer which advise the soul to enter within itself: and that is exactly what this means. . . . As far as I can understand, the door of entry into this castle is prayer and meditation.[2]

The Interior Castle was written during a period of about six months in the year 1577 as a spiritual guide for a group of nuns who were St. Teresa's "disciples." But very soon after its publication, it became widely known as a work of great spiritual wisdom, not only for the religious (there were hundreds of monasteries and convents in Spain in St. Teresa's day). But also for untold numbers of lay people was well. Steadily it was spread by re-publication and translation into many languages, and for centuries now it has been treasured throughout the world as one of the great classics of the spiritual life. Few books give as keen and detailed an analysis of Christian experience, from the time of the soul's awakening, through all its struggles, defeats, and victories, until it reaches the very portals of heaven.

Teresa was born in Avila, in central Spain, in 1515. Teresa was the daughter of well-to-do and noble parents, and she felt the drawing of God upon her heart early in life. Before she was twenty, she entered a Carmelite convent. But she was not really happy there. Her heart was not at peace. A long and severe illness caused her to become paralyzed for about two years. A period of deep inward struggle followed, lasting for years. In her autobiography she writes of that time,

> On the one hand God was calling me. On the other, I was following the world. All the things of God gave me pleasure, yet I was tied and bound to those of the world. It seemed as if I wanted to reconcile these two contradictory things, . . .the life of the spirit and the pleasures and joys and pastimes of the senses. . . . I spent nearly twenty years on that stormy sea, often falling in this way and each time rising again, but to little purpose, as I would only fall once more.[3]

Not until she was forty did the conflict cease. Then one day as she was praying before the statue of Christ being scourged, a new peace came to her, and a new and deeper life of prayer. Visions came too, and voices and seasons of rapturous ecstasy. It was the beginning of a continuing mystical experience for her. In her own analysis of these experiences, however, she always minimized any emphasis on visions or ecstatic states. For her, what mattered most was always the soul's surrender to God and walk with God, in humility and faith.

Teresa's experiences with God in her own life led her to be impatient with the spiritual laxity that prevailed in the convents of her order. She was convinced that without discipline the spiritual life is sure to suffer. So during the latter part of her life, Teresa led a far-reaching movement for reform in the Carmelite Order. She put into force again many of the order's original principles and practices. Her followers and the convents she founded and led (sixteen in all) were called the Carmelites of the Discalced and Primitive Order. In this effort to reform she often encountered bitter opposition and persecution. But she prevailed. Whether the specific practices she advocated (for example, going barefoot) would be approved today is less important than the spirit she exemplified and sought to impart. This spirit is expressed powerfully and beautifully in her four books, *The Way of Perfection*, *The Book of Foundations*, *The Life*, and *The Interior Castle*. The last was written only a few years before her death and embodied her mature thought in the most ordered form. This book, Evelyn Underhill says, "is full of Teresa's own bracing spirit, her dislike of all pretensions, all seeking for consolations, all idle and dreamy enjoyments, all spiritual conceit."[4] It is one of the world's masterpieces of spirituality.

One of the most remarkable things about Teresa of Avila was that she was able to combine the highest degree of inward spiritual experience with the greatest practical ability in dealing with human affairs. Prayer and administration were her forte and her pleasure. "She could turn from directions about the finances of the community or the right sweeping down of the house, to deal in a manner equally wise and precise with the most delicate problems of the soul."[5] Her books, filled with spiritual wisdom, were written in the intervals in her administrative work and her tiring journeys as a founder and reformer of religious houses. She herself was a remarkable combination of Mary and Martha, a combination she urgently recommended to her followers in her description of the Seventh Mansion.

The Interior Castle (or as it is commonly called in the Spanish editions, *The Mansions*) remains St. Teresa's greatest book, both because of its finished form and because of its depth of spiritual understanding. The basic symbolism of the "castle made up of a single diamond, having many rooms" permits her to deal with the problems of the spiritual life at every level, from the soul's first trembling response to the voice of God, to the highest reaches of prayer and contemplation.

Before considering some of the teachings of *The Interior Castle*, it is important to recall that it was written for the instruction of a group of nuns who were already members of the convent community. St. Teresa, with her long experience and keen insight into human psychology and spirituality, knew well that many people who had entered the "religious" life had really only taken the first few steps along with way of Christ. There were many "mansions" for them yet to enter in their quest of Christlike perfection. St. Teresa is surely right when she urges them not to be content to be merely "within the castle walls."

St. Teresa's analysis and portrayal of the various stages of spiritual development may at times seem to be somewhat mechanical or overdone. But we may be sure that she did not intend them to be interpreted too literally or legalistically. We might say that the stages described are meant to be *suggestive*, not *normative*.

In the First Mansion, we are given a vivid picture of the state of the soul at the beginning of its pilgrimage:

> The soul is still absorbed in worldly affairs . . . and puffed up by worldly honors and ambitions. There are so many bad things—snakes and vipers and poisonous creatures—which have come in with the soul that they prevent it from seeing the light. . . . These wild beasts and animals force him to close his eyes to everything but themselves.[6]

In the Second Mansion, the soul has begun to practice prayer, but not with full diligence. And it has not learned to avoid occasions of sin, "which is a very perilous condition." But God is continuing to call these souls, and St. Teresa says,

> As they gradually get nearer to the place where His Majesty dwells, He becomes a very good Neighbor to them. And even when we are engaged in worldly pastimes and businesses and pleasures and hagglings, when we are falling into sins and rising from them against—in spite of all that . . . He calls us ceaselessly, time after time, to approach Him. . . .
>
> His appeals come through the conversations of good people, or from sermons, or through the reading of good books. . . . Or they come through sickness and trials, or by means of truth which God teaches us at times when we are engaged in prayer.[7]

The Third Mansion shows the soul struggling with minor ethical problems, and still not finding great joy or freedom in prayer. In the Fourth Mansion, however, it begins to attain a higher level of prayer— prayer less dependent on its own efforts and activities and more on the indwelling work of God's Spirit in the heart. To make clear the meaning of this higher type of prayer, St. Teresa uses this helpful illustration:

> To understand [the prayer of quiet] better, let us suppose that we are looking at two fountains the basins of which can be filled with water. . . . These two large basins can be filled with water in different ways: the water in the one comes from a long distance, by means of numerous conduits and through human skill; but the other has been constructed at the very source of the water and fills without making any noise.[8]

The water from the first of these fountains, explains St. Teresa, "corresponds to the spiritual sweetness which is produced by meditation" (in other words, by our own spiritual efforts). To the second fountain, the water comes directly from its source, which is God. And when "He is pleased to grant us some supernatural favor, its coming is accompanied by the greatest peace and quietness and sweetness within ourselves."[9]

In other words, St. Teresa teaches that there is a higher level of prayer where, as it were, not we but the Spirit of God speaks in our hearts. This is in harmony with Paul's teaching in Romans 8, but perhaps all too few Christians enter into this experience. St. Teresa reminds us that this too is a gift, not a human achievement. "However many tears we shed, we cannot produce this water in those ways; it is given only to whom God wills to give it and often when the soul is not thinking of it at all."[10]

Going a step further to the Fifth Mansion, in her most famous metaphor St. Teresa likens the soul to an ugly crawling silkworm, which is enabled to build a cocoon where it is to die—but which then comes forth as a beautiful soaring white butterfly. By the transforming power of the Holy Spirit, it has been purified and set free into a wondrous new life with God:

> It sets no store by the things it did when it was a worm. . . . It has wings now: how can it be content to crawl along slowly when it is able to fly? All that it can do for God seems to it slight by comparison with its desires.[11]

The soul has found a new life of liberty, but it is still far from its goal. There are struggles and temptations yet to be overcome—some blatant and horrid, others subtle and difficult to detect—before it finally reaches fullness of peace. But the Spirit continually leads on, guiding, warning, strengthening, encouraging. In the Sixth Mansion, the soul's faith and love are more stabilized. Prayer has become very precious, and it finds joy in doing the will of God, no matter how difficult. But it also endures new trials. Often it is misunderstood even by close associates, who doubt its sincerity. "How holy she's getting!" they exclaim.[12] Nevertheless it presses on, calmly, bravely, and at last—sometimes after years (there are *eleven* chapters in the Sixth Mansion!)—it attains to the beatitude of the Seventh Mansion.

Now the soul is at peace. It has entered into the Spiritual Marriage, the life of union with God. Storms and temptations may rage around it, but peace abides within—the peace that passes all understanding. Concerning the new levels of prayer experienced in this blessed state St. Teresa writes,

> The Lord appears in the center of the soul . . . just as He appeared to the Apostles, without entering through the door, when He said to them, "Pax vobis!" This instantaneous communication of God to the soul is so great a secret and so sublime a favor, and such a delight is felt by the soul, that I do not know with what to compare it, beyond saying that the Lord is pleased to manifest to the soul at that moment the glory that is in Heaven, in a more sublime manner than is possible through any vision or spiritual consolation.[13]

But even here the soul must cling to God if it is to be kept secure. St. Teresa makes it clear that she does not teach "sinless perfection." As long as the soul is in the world, it is not beyond the possibility of temptation and sin:

> I may seem to be giving the impression that, when the soul reaches the state in which God grants it this favor, it is sure of its salvation and free from the risk of backsliding. But that is not my meaning.[14]

The times of trial and suffering are not past; yet peace reigns within. So complete is this peace of God that guards the heart that even opposition and persecution only serve to deepen it:

> When these souls are persecuted again, they have a great interior joy. . . . They bear no enmity with those who ill treat them, or desire to do so. Indeed they conceive a special love for them.[15]

The ideal of Christian sanctification portrayed in these quotations is so exalted that we are tempted to ask, "Who is sufficient for these things?" St. Teresa knows well that by no means all Christians will achieve the peace and victory of the Seventh Mansion. But she also knows the secret of such prevailing spiritual victory: it is the vision and companionship of Christ:

Fix your eyes on the Crucified and nothing else will be of much importance to you. . . . Do you know when people really become spiritual?
It is when they become slaves of God and are branded with his sign,
which is the sign of the Cross, in token that they have given Him their
freedom. Then He can sell them as slaves to the whole world, as he
Himself was sold.[16]

Through the teachings of *The Interior Castle* we are led into the deep-
est valleys and to the highest summits of spiritual experience. As we read
we marvel at both the purity and the author's spirit and the sublimity of
her words. Much of the time, especially in the later mansions, she seems
far beyond us. but when we falter or grow discouraged, it is good
to know that she also lived by an utterly simple faith, expressed in her
beautiful and often quoted poem:

Let nothing disturb thee,
Nothing affright thee;
All things are passing;
Good never changeth;
Patient endurance
Attaineth to all things;
Who God possesseth
In nothing is wanting;
Alone God sufficeth.[17]

7

The Book of Common Prayer

Anonymous

. . . that all who profess and call themselves Christians may be led into the way of truth, and hold the faith in unity of spirit, in the bond of peace, and in righteousness of life.

No other devotional book has molded the religious life of a whole nation as much as *The Book of Common Prayer* of the Church of England. Its influence, both religious and literary, has been second only to that of the King James Bible. Since the Church of England is "established," its official forms of public prayer and worship are prescribed by law. Thus the forms and words of *The Book of Common Prayer* become familiar from childhood to the great majority of the British people. But its world-wide use is by no means due only to prescription. Through more than four centuries this prayer book has become precious to a host of readers, not only in the Anglican (Episcopal) churches throughout the world, but also among many other Protestant denominations as well. Among Roman Catholics too the book has many fans, in part because it is largely derived from medieval worship forms. And it has been translated, in whole or in part, into more than 150 languages or dialects.

The Book of Common Prayer (or Prayer Book) has been slightly modified in the various Anglican churches, but these changes have been minor. The American prayer book, adopted in 1789, reflects the political changes that had come with independence, but also states clearly that "this church is far from intending to depart from the Church of England in any essential point of doctrine, discipline or worship."[1] The same would be true of the other Anglican prayer book versions in other countries. Throughout the world, the Prayer Book remains both a bulwark of the faith and a treasured guide for the spiritual life. Bishop Robert E. L. Strider has well expressed the high esteem in which it is held:

> To those who know and love it, the Prayer Book is not only a precious heritage from the Christian ages, enshrining in terms of lovely human speech the best men have thought about God, freedom and human destiny, but it is also a practical manual of worship public and private and a well-tested guide to all who would know and serve God more truly. . . . It makes ever fresh appeal to generations of Churchmen as they come and go.[2]

The first edition of *The Book of Common Prayer*, largely the work of Archbishop Thomas Cranmer, was published in 1549 in the reign of King Edward VI. Subsequently there were several other editions, with minor amendments, yielding to strong Catholic pressure under Queen Mary I, returning to more Protestant forms under Queen Elizabeth I, and reflecting a slight Puritan influence from the Commonwealth period. The form finally approved in 1662 has remained essentially unchanged, though various larger and smaller revisions have been proposed.

Archbishop Cranmer wanted to give to his people (in their own language, and in one volume) the chief liturgical treasure of the medieval church—purged of those teachings that had gradually sprung up through the centuries but had no true basis in Scripture. Concerning Cranmer's high achievement, Anglican scholar Percy Dearmer has said,

Cramer stands apart. . . . He was able to bring his own great gift to the Reformation—a power of liturgical art which places him among the great prose writers of the world. Others worked with him and after him, as others had worked before, and the beauty of their united product is a witness to the greatness of that age of literature which covered the hundred years between the first Prayer Book and the last, and gave us Shakespeare, Bacon, and Milton . . . and the Authorized Version of the Bible.[3]

The Prayer Book maintains a style that is always clear and beautiful, often noble and sublime. While at times the sixteenth-century language may impress us as having a slightly old-fashioned flavor, like the Authorized Version of the Bible, only seldom does this interfere with our understanding, and often it adds to the spiritual impact.

The literary qualities of *The Book of Common Prayer* are, however, not the most important. The basic reason for its worldwide and enduring appeal is unquestionably its thoroughly biblical character. From beginning to end, in both thought and language, it is based upon Scripture. In fact, approximately two-thirds consist of quotations from the Bible. And the remaining material, the prayers, the orders of worship, the occasional services, and even the creeds of the catechism, are cast largely in scriptural wording. It could almost be said that the Prayer Book is the Bible arranged and paraphrased for devotional use.

Closely related to the biblical character of the Prayer Book is the fact that it is churchly in its whole spirit and orientation. Its authors, rather than simply devising new forms, drew freely upon more than 1,500 years of the worship experience of the church. The result is a work of profound, tested spiritual substance. The devotional life it recommends is not of any individualistic sort. It is *the* book of common prayer. Its major services of prayer are intended to be conducted when the people of God are assembled in God's house. Both the festival and the occasional services presuppose the leadership of an ordained minister. This does not preclude larger participation by the laity, both in the reading of the Scriptures and in prayer and song. Nor does it make other, informal meetings, unnecessary. The point is rather that the basic devotional pattern of the Prayer Book is definitely church oriented. The Christian is to find his or her way forward, and homeward, not alone but among the people.

Finally, another reason for the universal appeal of *The Book of Common Prayer* is its comprehensive character. It provides forms and patterns of worship for many diverse occasions and needs: the public worship service; the administration of the sacraments; the "landmark occasions" of birth, baptism, confirmation, marriage, death, and burial; family prayers; the ordination of pastors and the consecration of bishops. There are prayers for the dying, and an order for anointing in illness. And the book certainly finds much of its usefulness in the believer's private devotions, though it was not written with this as a chief purpose. It is a book for all seasons and for all Christians. Not all Christians, however, will find it immediately appealing and devotionally satisfying. In both style and content it is more conservative than contemporary. To follow its guidance is basically not an emotional experience. It is rather like coming into a great cathedral where solemn music is being played, or like experiencing a true friendship, which ripens with the years.

As to the relative appeal of the various parts of the Prayer Book, there are different tastes and preferences, but, the hundreds of prayers throughout the volume have been widely cherished. Some are parts of worship services; many are designated for a certain Sunday or feast day; others stand alone, usually with titles indicating their appropriate use. There are prayers suited to almost every occasion and circumstance in life, each reflecting some aspect of the person's quest for God and life with God.

Among the many examples that might be given of especially inspiring prayers, here are some of the best known and loved:

A Collect for Grace

O Lord, our heavenly Father, Almighty and everlasting God, who hast safely brought us to the beginning of this day; defend us in the same with thy mighty power; and grant that this day we fall into no sin, neither run into any kind of danger; but that all our doings, being ordered by thy governance, may be righteous in thy sight; through Jesus Christ our Lord. Amen.[4]

The General Thanksgiving

Almighty God, Father of all mercies, we, thine unworthy servants, do give thee most humble and hearty thanks for all thy goodness and loving-kindness to us, and to all men. We bless thee for our creation, preservation, and all the blessings of this life; but above all, for thine inestimable love in the redemption of the world by our Lord Jesus Christ; for the means of grace, and for the hope of glory. And, we beseech thee, give us that due sense of all thy mercies, that our hearts may be unfeignedly thankful; and that we show forth thy praise, not only with our lips, but in our lives, by giving up our selves to thy service, and by walking before thee in holiness and righteousness all our days; through Jesus Christ our Lord, to whom, with thee and the Holy Ghost, be all honour and glory, world without end. Amen.[5]

The Collect for the Second Sunday in Advent

Blessed Lord, who hast caused all holy Scriptures to be written for our learning; Grant that we may in such wise hear them, read, mark, learn, and inwardly digest them, that by patience and comfort of thy holy Word, we may embrace, and ever hold fast, the blessed hope of everlasting life, which thou hast given us in our Saviour Jesus Christ. Amen.[6]

The Guidance

O God, by whom the meek are guided in judgment, and light riseth up in darkness for the godly; Grant us, in all our doubts and uncertainties, the grace to ask what thou wouldst have us to do, that the Spirit of Wisdom may save us from all false choices, and that in thy light we may see light, and in thy straight path may not stumble; through Jesus Christ our Lord. Amen.[7]

At Night

O Lord, support us all the day long, until the shadows lengthen and the evening comes, and the busy world is hushed, and the fever of life is over, and our work is done. Then in thy mercy grant us a safe lodging, and a holy rest, and peace at the last. Amen.[8]

Sometimes these question are raised: Is it really a healthy practice to use set forms of prayers? Shouldn't all of our prayers be spontaneous, arising directly out of the needs of our own hearts? Surely much of our prayer should be in our own words, but the long experience of Christians tells us that there is room and need for both types.

To quote Percy Dearmer again:

> There is some loss in the use of printed words, but there is greater gain. We have in them the accumulated wisdom and beauty of the Christian Church, the garnered excellence of many saints. We are by them released from the accidents of time and place. Above all we are preserved against the worst dangers of selfishness: in the common prayer we join together in a great fellowship that is as wide as the world; and we are guided, not by the limited notions of our own minister, nor by the narrow impulses of our own desires, but by the mighty voice that rises from the general heart of Christendom.[9]

Much of *The Book of Common Prayer* is taken up with forms for public worship, and these too are beautiful, thought-stirring, and edifying. For many of us they will differ considerably from the forms to which we are most accustomed. But even when this is so, a common note of humility, awe, thanksgiving, and petition pervades all the forms of true worship, including these. The liturgies contained in *The Book of Common Prayer* are largely rooted in the worship practices of past centuries. Praying these "common prayers," even the most unconventional and informal of Christians scarcely fail to experience as did the psalmist of old that *"strength* and *beauty* are in thy sanctuary."

One of the very useful parts of *The Book of Common Prayer*, which might easily be overlooked, is the division of the Psalter into readings for morning and evening prayer for each day of a month. The Psalms never wear out. The monks used to chant the whole Psalter every week. *The Book of Common Prayer* makes the task easier for us by distributing it over a whole month. The version of the Psalms in the Prayer Book differs somewhat from the King James, but in most instances this only adds to the reader's interest.

The appointed epistle and Gospel readings, arranged for all the Sundays and holy days, comprise a very important section making up more than one-fourth of the entire Prayer Book. It gathers up the treasured usages of ages past, and following the worship pattern of the church year, provide an ever-renewed source of grace and spiritual enrichment. The texts are those generally followed in the liturgical churches. A complete table of daily scripture readings is also provided, covering practically the entire Bible in a year, with some of the greatest passages read at least twice. *The Book of Common Prayer* is indeed a guide and companion to all the Scriptures and along every way of life.

In the church of Christ, there is "one Body and one Spirit, one Lord, one faith, one baptism, one God and Father of all." But there are still many divisions and denominations. Christ still prays: "That they all may be one." Ecumenism is still a largely unattained goal, though now that goal seems to be coming nearer. Through *The Book of Common Prayer* we gratefully receive the riches of one of the great traditions of Christendom, and look forward to the fuller realization of "one Body and one Spirit," we may fittingly pray:

> O God, who hast made of one blood all nations of men for to dwell on the face of the whole earth, and didst send thy blessed Son to preach peace to them that are far off and to them that are nigh; Grant that all men everywhere may seek after thee and find thee. Bring the nations into thy fold, pour out thy Spirit upon all flesh, and hasten thy kingdom; though the same thy Son Jesus Christ our Lord. Amen.[10]

THE SETTING: 17th-century France
THE BOOK: A humble kitchen worker shares the secret of unbroken fellowship with God

8

The Practice of the Presence of God

Brother Lawrence

The time of business does not with me
differ from the time of prayer.

In the fields of both science and religion, great forward steps have usually been the result of a new, sometimes startling, insight into a previously unknown truth. Often this is expressed in a simplified statement of that truth: that the earth and other planets revolve around the sun, that lightning is a form of electricity, that some substances are radioactive. In the field of science such insights usually come as a result of great learning. The discoverers were people of wide knowledge and keen intellect, if not genius.

In the field of religion, however, while many of the great pioneers were people of both outstanding talent and thorough education, often this was not so. Moses trained in the learning of the Egyptians and Isaiah lived at court, but Amos and Micah were men from the countryside. Paul was well educated, but Peter and several of the other apostles were fishermen. George Fox was an unschooled tailor; D. L. Moody was a shoe clerk; Richard Allen, the founder and leader of the African Methodist Episcopal Church, was a former slave who had purchased his own freedom.

Among the host of unlettered prophets who have enriched the life of the church through important spiritual insight or leadership, one of the most unforgettable figures is Carmelite brother Nicholas Herman, best known by his monastic name, Brother Lawrence. His teachings concerning the practice of the presence of God strike a key note that has made him an unobtrusive but exceedingly effective teacher of many generations of Christians.

It would be hard to imagine a life course less promising than that of Brother Lawrence: born and raised in poverty, receiving only the most meager education, serving as a soldier and a household servant; finally, dissatisfied with what life had had to offer, entering a monastery and being assigned to the most menial duties in the kitchen. Yet in the humble setting he steadily "grew in favor with God and men," so that in his later years he was sought out for his spiritual counsel by many of the prominent church leaders of Paris. After Brother Lawrence's death, a friend who was vicar to one of the Parisian prelates was authorized to publish notes from some of Brother Lawrence's conversations, adding to them a number of his letters. Together they form only a slender volume, but within its few pages are distilled precious lessons concerning the heart of the spiritual life.

In the 300 years since Brother Lawrence's death, *The Practice of the Presence of God* has been reprinted again and again, translated into many languages, and prized by Catholics and Protestants alike. It has been circulated throughout the world. Perhaps a chief secret of its popularity is the unadorned beauty of Brother Lawrence's own life, which clearly shines through its simple pages. The preface to one edition gives this characterization of the author:

A wholly consecrated man, he lived his life as if he were a singing pilgrim on the march, as happy in serving his fellow monks and brothers from the monastery kitchen as in serving God in the vigil of prayer and penance. He died at eighty years of age, full of love and years and honored by all who knew him, leaving a name which has been as "precious ointment poured forth."[1]

Born in 1611 in Lorraine, France, Nicholas Herman was already past middle life when he joined the barefooted Carmelites and was assigned to his kitchen duties. Those duties were at first very distasteful to him: he says he was "a clumsy fellow who broke everything." Likewise, he had little taste for the business dealings sometimes connected with his work. But he accepted all of it as God's will for him, and he gradually gained the great insight he later so gladly taught to others: that God is present in even the most commonplace of circumstance. Brother Lawrence himself spent his whole life, thenceforth, as a "servant of the servants of God" among the pots and kettles. He died in 1691 when he was eighty.

The heart of Brother Lawrence's message, given in the very title of *The Practice of the Presence of God*, is concisely stated in a passage in the first letter:

Having found in many books different methods of going to God, the diverse practices of the spiritual life, I thought this would serve rather to puzzle me than facilitate what I sought after, which was nothing but how to become wholly God's. This made me resolve to give all for the all; so after having given myself wholly to God, that He might take away my sin, I renounced, for the love of Him, everything that was not He, and I began to live as if there was none but He and I in the world. Sometimes I considered myself before Him as a poor criminal before his judge; at other times I beheld Him in my heart as my Father, as my God. . . . I worshipped Him the oftenest that I could, keeping my mind in His Holy presence, and recalling it as often as I found it wandered from Him. . . . I continued it . . . without troubling or disquieting myself when my mind had wandered involuntarily. I made this my business as much all the day long as at the appointed times of prayer; for at all times, every hour, every minute, even in the height of my business, I drove away from my mind everything that was capable of interrupting my thought of God.[2]

The profound truths contained in this letter were not the result of a single experience, however. They grew out of a background of many years of walking with God. The beginnings of his conversion, he tells us, came when he was eighteen years of age. His account is reported in the first recorded conversation:

> In the winter, seeing a tree stripped of its leaves, and considering that within a little time the leaves would be renewed, and after that the flowers and fruit appear, he received a high view of the providence and power of God, which has never since been effaced from his soul. This view had perfectly set him loose from the world and kindled in him such a love for God that he could not tell whether it had increased during the more than forty years he had lived since.[3]

He did not come to full spiritual clarity at once. Although he wanted to love and serve God, for ten years his faith was wavering and marked by inward struggle. Then suddenly he was set free:

> For the first ten years, I suffered much. . . . During this time I fell often, and rose again presently. . . . When I thought of nothing but to end my days in these troubles . . . I found myself changing all at once; and my soul . . . felt a profound inward peace, as if she were in her center and place of rest.[4]

This spiritual liberation set him free, too, from any slavish devotion to religious forms. He learned to rejoice in God alone:

> I have quitted all forms of devotion and set prayers but those to which my state obliges me. And I make it my business only to persevere in His holy presence, wherein I keep myself by a simple attention, and a general fond regard to God, which I may call an actual *presence* of God.[5]

Although he constantly found God in his work, Brother Lawrence's religion was by no means one of "works," but thoroughly evangelical:

> All possible kinds of mortification, if they were void of the love of God, could not efface a single sin. We ought, without anxiety, to expect the pardon of our sins from the blood of Jesus Christ, only endeavoring to love him with all our hearts.[6]

For Brother Lawrence, work and prayer became parts of one unified pattern of life. In addition to its central and often reiterated emphasis on practicing the presence, Brother Lawrence's book has a number of important subordinate teachings regarding the Christian life. One of these, seen especially in the letters, points to the singular beauty of true Christian friendship. He is concerned with giving counsel regarding the practical problems of illness, doubt, loneliness. But whether he writes to men or women, breathing through these letters is a spirit of warm, Christ-centered friendship. One of its constant expressions is mutual intercessory prayer, simply, directly, asked for and given: "Pray to Him for me as I pray to Him for you. I hope to see Him quickly."[7]

Another strong impression made by Brother Lawrence is his complete freedom from dogmatism. His theological views are orthodox, but he does not stress them. Faith for him is a practical matter, rooted in his own experience of the grace of God, tested and proved in everyday life. He is not at all interested in winning anyone else to his theology. His book does not contain a single direct quotation of Scripture. Yet the light of Christ and the life in Christ shine through it all. This wholly indirect approach to the dogmas of religion is certainly one of the secrets of Brother Lawrence's universal appeal.

The reader cannot fail to note, too, that despite its very elementary subject matter and its complete lack of literary pretense, *The Practice of the Presence* has many singularly apt phrases characterizing the spiritual life: we are to serve God "with a holy freedom";[8] our fellowship with God is "a commerce of love";[9] as his friends we are invited "to eat at the King's table";[10] we are urged to enter into "the oratory of the heart";[11] we must "give all for all";[12] "those who have the gale of the Holy Spirit go forward even in sleep."[13] Brother Lawrence does not think abstractly, but practically, and for him the practice of the presence of God is a quiet symphony of service, faith, and love.

And his vision of God, intertwining and uniting all aspects of his life, remains clear, unbroken, persistent to the end. To an elderly friend stricken with illness, he writes in one of his last letters,

> He requires no great matters of us: . . . a little adoration; sometimes to pray for his grace, sometimes to offer him your sufferings, and sometimes to return Him thanks for the favours he has given you, and still gives you, in the midst of your troubles. . . .

Lift up your heart to Him, sometimes even at your meals, and when you are in company; the least little remembrance will always be acceptable to Him. . . . It is not necessary for being with God to be always at church. We may make an oratory of our heart wherein to retire from time to time to converse with him in meekness, humility and love. . . . Let us begin, then. . . . Have courage. We have but little time to live; you are near sixty-four, and I am almost eighty. Let us live and die with God.[14]

Lacking a formal education and deprived of most advantages, Brother Lawrence's life has nevertheless flowed out in blessing for all subsequent generations. No one knows how many editions there have been of his little book, nor how many millions have read his words. but the ever-widening influence of his life clearly exemplifies his own statement: "When [God] finds a soul penetrated with a living faith, he pours into it his graces and favors plentifully; there they flow like a torrent which . . . spreads itself with impetuosity and abundance."[15]

In Brother Lawrence the prophecy of Joel, quoted by Peter on the Day of Pentecost, finds striking fulfillment: "Even upon the menservants and maidservants in those days I will pour out my spirit" (Joel 2:29). And the ancient prophetic word that Christ applied to all his followers is surely also fulfilled in this, his humble disciple: "They shall all be taught by God" (John 6:45).

9

Pilgrim's Progress

John Bunyan

GREAT-HEART: But here was great odds, three against one.
VALIANT-FOR-TRUTH: 'Tis true; but little or more are
nothing to him that has the truth on his side.

Many of the world's great books have been written in prison. The apostle Paul and the philosopher Boethius, Sir Walter Raleigh and Mahatma Gandhi, Dietrich Bonhoeffer and Martin Luther King Jr., and a host of others have penned undying messages from prison cells. Among these writings, one of the most renowned and beloved is *Pilgrim's Progress* by John Bunyan. The most famous allegory in English literature, it portrays the Christian life as a long and hazardous journey from the City of Destruction to the heavenly Zion. In the course of his narrative, Bunyan creates hundreds of characters and scenes that have become everyday words and themes. Few books in all the world have been translated and republished more often. It is a true religious classic, speaking to the heart of everyone on an "inward pilgrimage" through the world.

John Bunyan was a Baptist minister in seventeenth-century England, a time of much religious persecution. He was born at Elstow in central

England in 1628, of poor parents, and he received very little education. John's remarkable mastery of English seems to have come chiefly from the Bible. For a time he worked as a brazier, the same occupation as his father. Then for about two years, in Cromwell's time, he served in the army. During this early period he lived a careless and openly ungodly life. Around 1649 he married "a woman of piety," and it was especially through two books she recommended that he was led to faith and newness of life in Christ. He became a member of the church in Bedford, and in 1659 he began his preaching ministry which, except for his prison years, continued throughout his life and extended at times to many parts of England. Other than these few facts, we know little of his personal life, except that he spent many years in jail for preaching without a license. He died in 1688.

We do know, however, that John Bunyan was, as part of the English Baptist tradition, always a great lover of liberty. Roger Williams, who first established religious freedom in an American colony, and William Carey, the father of modern missions, were a part of this same tradition. And Bunyan, in his later ministry, showed himself a true defender of religious liberty by advocating the practice of "open church membership"—admitting those who practiced infant baptism as well as those who did not. He wrote many books, including his autobiography, *Grace Abounding to the Chief of Sinners*. But only *Pilgrim's Progress* has endured. It has won fame and acclaim, not only for its literary style and its imaginative genius, but above all for its symbolic portrayal of the varieties of Christian experience. Christians of every denomination and of every station in life find their own hearts and experiences reflected again and again along the pilgrim's way. One contemporary writer describes its universal appeal in these words: "This book has been read in prim parlors, in sophisticated drawing rooms, in royal households, in religion classes, in public schools, in family worship—and will be read forever."[1]

Pilgrim's Progress is written in two parts, "under the similitude of a dream." In Part I the author lies down to sleep in a "den" (representing Bedford jail), and in his dream he catches his first glimpse of the pilgrim:

> I dreamed, and behold I saw a man clothed with rags, standing in a certain place, with his face from his own house, a book in his hand, and a great burden upon his back. I looked, and saw him open the book, and read therein; and as he read, he wept and trembled; and, not being able longer to contain, he broke out in a lamentable cry, saying, "What shall I do?"[2]

The pilgrim's family members are of no help to him; rather, they make light of his trouble and seek to hinder him from leaving his home in the City of Destruction. But his burden is heavy, and he is ready to do anything to be free of it. Walking one day in the fields, reading his book and deeply distressed in spirit, he encounters Evangelist, who advises him to flee, and gives him directions as to where he may find deliverance. He listens and sets forth. Soon he meets others, some of whom try to confuse and mislead him, but he does not permit himself to be distracted. Passing through the Wicket Gate, to which Evangelist has pointed him, and with further guidance from the Interpreter, he comes at length within sight of the cross of Christ. Here is Bunyan's unforgettable picture of a soul finding peace:

> Now, I saw in my dream that the highway up which Christian was to go was fenced on either side with a wall that was called Salvation. Up this way, therefore, did burdened Christian run, but not without great difficulty, because of the load on his back.

> He ran thus till he came to a place somewhat ascending; and upon that place stood a cross, and a little below, in the bottom, a sepulcher. So I saw in my dream, that just as Christian came up with the cross, his burden loosed from off his shoulders, and fell from off his back, and began to tumble, and so continued to do till it came to the mouth of the sepulcher, where it fell in, and I saw it no more.

> Then was Christian glad and lightsome, and said with a merry heart, "He hath given me rest by His sorrow, and life by his death."[3]

Following the portrayal of Christian's initial spiritual crisis and liberation, Bunyan continues to a wide variety of struggles, tribulations, defeats, and victories that mark the Christian way. Shortly after leaving home, he had met Obstinate and Pliable, representing contrasting false attitudes toward the claims of religion. Now he soon encounters Apollyon, the armored fiend from the Pit, who "made at him, throwing darts as thick as hail."[4] Christian is wounded, but the combat continues on for a half day. At one point Christian loses his sword, but then skillfully regains it, and finally gives Apollyon "a deadly thrust, which made him give back, as one that had received a mortal wound."[5]

A major source of help and blessing to Christian along his way is the friendship of two men who become his close companions: first Faithful, and then, after Faithful's tragic death, Hopeful. One day as he and Faithful are walking along together, they are joined by an apparent "fellow pilgrim" named Talkative, who is indeed very orthodox in his conversation, but full of empty words. When Faithful is beginning to be deceived, Christian enlightens him:

> This man with whom you are so taken will beguile with this tongue of his twenty of them that know him not. . . . He talketh of prayer, of repentance, of faith, and of the new birth; but he knows but only to talk of them. . . . His house is as empty of religion as the white of an egg is of savor.[6]

As Faithful continues his conversation with Talkative, the falsity of the latter's religion is clearly revealed. At the end he calls Faithful a "peevish or melancholy man not fit to be discoursed with,"[7] and leaves him. The pilgrims meet other characters who likewise seek to divert them from the truth. Atheist laughs at them when they say they are going to Mount Zion, a place he says does not even exist. Mr. Money-love gives a clever defense both of the minister who so manipulates things that he can get a better salary, and of the merchant who uses religion to improve his business. Ignorance is proud of his honesty and morality, but counsels the pilgrims to "follow the religion of your own country, and I will follow the religion of mine."[8] Objections and opposition to the Christian way take hundreds of different forms.

Arriving at Vanity Fair, a huge marketplace where all the goods and pleasures of the world are on display, the pilgrims do not conform to the ways of the patrons of the fair—neither in speech, nor in dress, nor in manner. They disparage both the "riches" and the activities going on around them. When they refuse to change, they are arrested and brought to trial before the judge, Lord Hate-Good. False witnesses accuse them, the jury finds them guilty, and Faithful, who has spoken out with special boldness, is condemned "to be put to the most cruel death that could be invented."[9] As Faithful dies, the author sees that "a chariot and a couple of horses carry him up through the clouds with sound of trumpet the nearest way to the Celestial Gate."[10] Christian is sent back to prison, but after a time is released.

Not long after these sad events, Christian is joined by Hopeful. They have good fellowship, but unfortunately they very soon yield to the temptation to turn off the highway through Bypath Meadow because the way there seems shorter. This leads to their capture by Giant Despair, who throws them into the dark dungeon of Doubting Castle. He flogs them mercilessly, showing them the bones of earlier pilgrims who have died at his hand, and at last tells them to commit suicide. In their misery they even consider this, but are deterred by the Word of God. After days of suffering, earnest prayer leads them to remember that they do have a Key of Promise that will open the doors of the castle. Thus they escape and are soon back on the King's Highway.

Not all the experiences of the pilgrims, however, involve temptation and suffering. Many people give them help and encouragement. Early in his journey, for instance, the pilgrim visits the House Beautiful, built by the Lord of the Hill for the relief and security of pilgrims. There he meets the three beautiful sisters, Piety, Prudence, and Charity, who bid him a warm welcome and invite him to be their guests for the evening meal and the night. They engage in long conversations, especially about the experiences Christian has had along the way. They also speak much of Christ and of what he has done for them:

PRUDENCE: And what makes you so desirous to go to Mount Zion?

CHRISTIAN: Why there I hope to see him alive that did hang dead upon the cross; and there I hope to be rid of all those things that to this day are any annoyance to me. There, they say, there is no death, and there I shall dwell with such company as I like best. For . . . I love Him because I was by Him eased of my burden.[11]

On the following day, the sisters show him many of the treasures of the House Beautiful and, persuading him to stay yet another day, direct his vision to the Delectable Mountains in Immanuel's Land in the distance. When he sets forth, he has been so strengthened and inspired by their Christian fellowship that he is able to face without fear the Valley of Humiliation and other perils of the way.

The journey is long. There are rugged mountains and fierce enemies, yet there are refreshing variations as well. Bunyan sketches a multitude of scenes, all interesting, all different, all showing keen psychological and spiritual insight. At last, after many years, Christian and Hopeful draw near to the Holy City. And like all pilgrims, they must pass through the dreaded River of Death. Bunyan depicts this experience vividly:

> They then addressed themselves to the water; and entering, Christian began to sink, and crying out to his good friend Hopeful, he said, "I sink in deep waters: the billows go over my head: all his waves are going over me. Selah." Then said the other, "Be of good cheer, my brother; I feel the bottom, and it is good." Then said Christian, "Ah, my friend, the sorrows of death have compassed me about." And with that, a great darkness and horror fell upon Christian.[12]

The two pilgrims in the river struggle on, at times almost completely overcome by doubt and terror. But they encourage each other by recalling some of the rich promises of Scripture, and are finally victorious. Christian "found ground to stand upon, and so it followed that the rest of the river was but shallow. Thus they got over."[13]

Part II of *Pilgrim's Progress* tells the parallel story of Christiana, Christian's wife, and her four children, who after a time also repent and set out on the way to the Celestial City. Early in their journey, Christina enlists a gentle pilgrim named Mercy, and they meet other helpful friends along the way too. Above all they have the companionship of a special guardian and guide named Great-Heart, the most inspiring character in the entire book, a symbol of the Holy Spirit.

Throughout Part II there is a strong emphasis on the blessings of Christian fellowship, symbolized by a group of pilgrims journeying together. Often they are refreshed and encouraged by other groups along the way. For a whole month they share the delightful hospitality of the House Beautiful. At the inn where Gaius is the host their conversation about "their Lord, themselves, and their journey" lasts through the entire night until daybreak. Even in the town of Vanity, where Faithful had been cruelly martyred, they are helped by a small but bold group, all of whom are also on the way to the Celestial City.

This second group of pilgrims visits many of the same places as Christian and his companions had, and they frequently encounters similar difficulties and joys. At times their conversations grow somewhat lengthy, but most of the time the narrative moves briskly with fresh examples of Bunyan's biblical symbolism. As an illustration of how strikingly he clothes profound spiritual truth in allegorical dress, we may

quote snatches of the conversation with Great-Heart as the pilgrims pass
through the Valley of Humiliation where Christian had his fierce battle
with Apollyon.

This valley is, above all, the place where pilgrims learn the grace
of humility. It is, therefore, despite the dangers lurking in shadows, a
very precious place, as we also learn from the pilgrim's conversation.
Great-Heart's opening words calm their fears, aroused by the news of
Christian's hard fight:

> We need not be afraid of this valley, for here is nothing to hurt us unless
> we procure it to ourselves. . . . It is the best and most fruitful ground in
> all these parts. . . . Behold how green this valley is, also how beautiful
> with lilies. I have also known many laboring men that have got good
> estates in this Valley of Humiliation, for "God resisteth the proud but
> giveth grace to the humble."[14]

As they go along conversing, they come upon a young lad watching
sheep. Suddenly they hear that he is singing and from his lips come the
words of one of Bunyan's most lovely hymns:

> He that is down needs fear no fall,
>   He that is low no pride;
> He that is humble, ever shall
>   Have God to be his guide.[15]

Great-Heart comments: "Do you hear him? I will dare to say that
this boy lives a merrier life, and wears more of the herb called heart's-
ease in his bosom than he that is clad in silk and velvet."[16] Continuing the
allegory, he goes on to say,

> In this valley our Lord formerly had his country house. He loved much
> to be here. He loved also to walk these meadows. . . . Besides, here a man
> shall be free from the noise and from the hurrying of this life. . . . This is
> a valley that nobody walks in but those that love a pilgrim's life.[17]

Mercy, Christiana's young companion, responds here, indicating the blessings and benefits that she has found in this valley:

> I think that I am as well in this valley as I have been anywhere else in all our journey; the place, methinks, suits with my spirit. Here one may . . . be thinking what he is, whence he came, what he has done, and to what the King has called him. . . . They that go rightly through this Valley of Baca make it a well; the rain that God sends down from heaven upon them that are here also filleth the pools.[18]

Great-Heart concludes and summarizes the conversations by quoting the promise of the Lord to Isaiah: "To this man will I look, even to him that is poor and of a contrite spirit"(Isaiah 66:2). No brighter jewel than humility adorns the Christian's crown, and in the symbolism of the Valley of Humiliation Bunyan graphically portrays it in all its loveliness.

Christiana and her companions reach the end of their journey after overcoming many obstacles and adversaries. One by one, they too are summoned to come to the Palace of the King. Each one responds in words of victorious, though at times trembling, faith. Mr. Valiant-for-Truth answers the summons with a matchless witness:

> "I am going to my Father's. . . . My sword I give to him that succeeds me in my pilgrimage, and my courage and skill to him that can get it. My marks and scars I carry with me, to be a witness for me that I have fought his battles who will now be my rewarder." So he passed over, and all the trumpets sounded for him on the other side.[19]

The final scene describes the crossing-over of Mr. Standfast, a noble pilgrim figure who has joined them late in their journey. The river at the moment is calm, and "when he was about half-way in [he] stood a while and talked to his companions."[20] He speaks of his great longing to come at last into the presence of Christ:

> I am going to see that head which was crowned with thorns, . . . and shall be with him in whose company I delight myself. I have loved to hear my Lord spoken of; and wherever I have seen the print of his shoe in the earth, there I have coveted to set my foot, too.[21]

Here is the authentic pilgrim spirit: complete devotion to the Savior, eagerness to follow wherever his footsteps lead, steadfastness through all the struggles of the way, to the end.

Throughout his whole presentation of the Christian's journey "from cross to crown," Bunyan's aim is not only to instruct and entertain, but also to challenge. The pilgrim way is long and rugged, often full of danger. But the resources of God are ever at hand. To overcome and safely arrive home at last, it is only necessary that we be willing to make the decisive choice, to set forth, to continue in the way. Mr. Valiant-for-Truth puts it best, in the words of Bunyan's now famous poem:

> He who would valiant be
> 'Gainst all disaster,
> Let him in constancy
> Follow the Master.
> There's no discouragement
> Shall make him once relent
> His first avowed intent
> To be a pilgrim. . . .
>
> Since, Lord, thou dost defend
> Us with thy Spirit,
> We know we at the end
> Shall life inherit.
> Then fancies flee away!
> I'll fear not what men say,
> I'll labor night and day
> To be a pilgrim.[22]

THE SETTING: 18th-century colonial America
THE BOOK: A Quaker tradesman-minister tells of his faith and his witness
against slavery and other social evils

10

The Journal of John Woolman

John Woolman

I have seen in the Light of the Lord that the day is approaching when the man that is most wise in human policy shall be the greatest fool; and the arm that is mighty to support injustice shall be broken in pieces.

John Woolman is perhaps the most eloquent and persuasive voice in 300 years of Quaker history in North America. His *Journal* is famous both as a document of social protest and as a masterpiece of American literature. Among the spiritual classics of the whole world it stands high because of its unique combining of the twofold call to devoted inner life with God and to a life of uncompromising justice and brotherhood toward people. But like the other classics, *The Journal of John Woolman* was the product of a single life. It was nurtured in the fertile soil of vital fellowship in the Society of Friends.

The Friends, or Quakers, had their beginnings in the middle of the seventeenth century in the preaching of George Fox, who was born in Fenny Drayton in central England, the son of a weaver. As a young man, Fox was burdened by an overwhelming sense of guilt. After seeking help from various religious leaders, but finding none, in great anguish of spirit he turned to seek God in his own heart. In his *Journal* he tells how he found peace:

> When all my hopes in them and in all men were gone, so that I had nothing outwardly to help me, . . . then I heard a voice which said, "There is one, even Christ Jesus, that can speak to thy condition." And when I heard it, my heart did leap for joy.[1]

In that moment the gospel of Christ became for George Fox not only a message written in the Bible and preached about in the church, but also a living reality within his own heart. Soon he began to preach, proclaiming the liberating power of Christ, which he himself had experienced, and opposing and denouncing the lax ways and "merely doctrinal" preaching prevalent in the churches. Followers gathered around him, attracted by his magnetic personality and his devoted life.

But before the Toleration Act of 1689, there was little religious freedom in England, and soon Fox and the Friends met persecution, arrest, and imprisonment. The Friends, however, were persistent. No persecution could dissuade them from obeying the Light of Christ that they had found. In addition, they strongly emphasized the practice of sincere love toward all people, regardless of creed or status. The latter conviction led them to the total renunciation of war, and to opposition to slavery and to every form of social injustice.

The first great Quaker leader in North America was William Penn, who in 1682 founded Pennsylvania as a colony based on Quaker principles, providing religious freedom for all who confessed their faith in God. Through the practice of brotherly love and understanding, Penn established friendly relations with the Native Americans so that Pennsylvania became in truth a "peaceable kingdom." But it was not to endure. Quakerism gradually grew more compromised in its practices, both in its relations with the Native Americans and in its attitudes toward slavery and many other social evils. It was in this setting that the quiet voice of John Woolman became a powerful prophetic witness, calling the Friends back to their true heritage of faith and practice. Woolman was born in 1720 in Northampton, New Jersey, and grew up in an atmosphere of simple, devout Quaker life. For a time he worked for a shopkeeper, while learning the trade of tailoring. After a while he was able to set up his own small business, which soon because quite prosperous and enabled him to give much of his time to traveling and preaching as a self-supported Quaker minister. This relatively independent status freed him to champion unpopular causes and protest against slavery, poverty, and other forms of oppression. And Woolman used his freedom well.

John Woolman's *Journal*, published in 1774, two years after his death, records the story of his life of spiritual ministry and social protest. He began to write it in 1756, when he was thirty-six years old, but it tells also of the experiences of his earlier childhood, of his quest for peace with God, and of his early awakening to the reality of the evils prevailing around him. The narrative quickly moves on to tell of his lifelong struggle against many forms of injustice. *The Journal* continues up until a few days before his death, which occurred in 1772. Through its simple, often quaint Quaker language, we are introduced to an unassuming but powerful life that was to make its mark upon the subsequent history of a whole nation. *The Journal* is not a large book, only a little more than 200 pages, but it turns the searchlight of truth on many issues and questions that have troubled the consciences of modern men and women across the globe.

The institution of slavery came to be a constant object of Woolman's attacks. In the long struggle against slavery, the words and witness of John Woolman are a shining light of hope and promise. And his *Journal* has a strangely contemporary quality today, when problems concerning war, race, and money deeply trouble the conscience of North America. Woolman spoke convincingly on all these issues. Moreover, he was profoundly concerned about all human suffering and injustice. The fear of God seems to have set him utterly free from the fear of humankind. He saw through the thinly veiled shallowness, injustice, and cruelty that most of his fellow citizens simple accepted or condoned.

In a sense, the life recorded in John Woolman's *Journal* was one of narrow compass. He did not travel far—except during his voyage to England, where he died. But he did go on many preaching trips, including one longer journey to the South. And everywhere he went, he engaged in a profound personal ministry. Custom and formality were never highly regarded by him either in daily life or in the religious sphere. He sought to bring people face to face with God and God's uncompromising claims. A few quotations reveal how bold and clear his thinking was.

Concerning slavery, Woolman's conscience was first awakened when, in his capacity as a public scrivener, he was asked to draft a bill of sale for a black slave. He did it, with great reluctance, but afterward he came to see slave holding as practice inconsistent with the Christian religion and vowed "Never again!" His first involvement was his last. Later, he writes,

> These are the people by whose labor the other inhabitants are in great measure supported, and many of them in the luxuries of life. These are the people who have made no agreement to serve us. . . . These are the souls for whom Christ died, and for our conduct toward them we must answer before Him who is no respector of persons.[2]

> Many slaves on this continent are oppressed, and their cries have reached the ears of the Most High! . . . Should we now . . . neglect to do our duty in firmness and constancy. . . . God may be terrible things in righteousness answer us this matter.[3]

Though gentle-hearted and kindly, John Woolman, when face to to face with evil, was as stern and uncompromising as truth. Regarding the injustices done to the Native Americans, Woolman's words are equally pointed:

> As I rode over the barren hills my meditations were on the alterations in the circumstances of the natives of this land since the coming in of the English. . . . The natives have in some places, for trifling considerations, sold their inheritance so favorably situated, and in other places have been driven back by superior force. . . . By the extension of English settlements. . . . the wild beasts on which the natives chiefly depend for subsistence are not so plentiful as they were, and people too often for the sake of gain, induce them to waste their skins and furs in purchasing a liquor which tends to the ruin of them and their families.[4]

But Woolman was disturbed by more than such flagrant evils. He became keenly aware of the temptations connected with increasing business enterprises, and after a time he decided to give up his mercantile business and continue only as a tailor, with no apprentices, in order a devote himself more undividedly to a spiritual service. He saw the dangers involved in all kinds of self-indulgence and luxuries. He noticed a common connection between the "too liberal use of spirituous liquors and custom of wearing too costly apparel" and vigorously opposed both.[5] As an earnest Quaker, he was of course a strong opponent of war and all violence, but he also understood that the causes of war were usually greed and a lust for power. Searchingly he asked himself, "Am I doing anything in my manner of life, that will ultimately have the effect of leading of war?" Whatever he found to have this result, he gave up.

In every area of life he prized and cultivated an unsullied conscience. Within his heart he struggled earnestly to see truth regarding every issue, and likewise in his actions never to compromise what he had come to see was right.

Some might say that he was over-scrupulous. Once, for example, when he contemplated a trip to the West Indies to look into the condition of the black slaves there, he felt he could not accept passage at the lower fare that was made possible by the illicit trade carried on by these vessels. He gave up the use of sugar because it was produced by slave labor. He wore simple clothes because he saw that luxurious dress often led to pride and conflict. He prayed to the Lord on behalf of the Friends "that He would graciously lead some to be patterns of deep self-denial in things relating to trade and handcraft labor; and that others who have plenty of the treasure of this world may be examples of a plain frugal life, and pay wages to such as they may hire more liberally than is customary in some places."[6]

And in a similar vein, he wrote to Friends in North Carolina who were subjected to the twin temptations of slave-holding and a too strong desire for profit:

> Take heed that no view of outward gain get too deep hold on you, that so your eyes being single to the Lord, you may be preserved in the way of safety. Where people let loose their minds after the love of outward things and are more engaged in pursing the profits than to be inwardly acquainted with the way of true peace, they walk in a vain shadow.[7]

Always, too, although his own conscience was keen and sensitive, Woolman was anxious to have the judgment of other Christians. After his struggle about accepting passage to the West Indies, he went back to his home community in Philadelphia to seek further counsel. In quaint Quaker words he says,

> In the fresh spring of pure love I had some labors in a private way among Friends on a subject relating to truth's testimony. . . . And I was graciously helped to discharge my duty in the fear and dread of the Almighty.[8]

Sensitive to the guidance of the Spirit, Woolman paid attention also to his dreams as possible channels of God's speaking to him. In a famous passage in The *Journal*, written in England shortly before his death, he recalls how a few years earlier he had been critically ill with pleurisy, so ill that he could not even remember his own name. Then, through his feverish imaginings, there came to him a symbolic vision of the meaning and message of his life. Here is how he described it:

> Being then desirous to know who I was, I saw a mass of matter of dull gloomy color, between the south and the east, and was informed that this mass was human beings in as great misery as they could be, and live, and that I was mixed with them, and that henceforth I might not consider myself as a distinct or separate being. In this state I remained several hours. I was then carried in spirit to the miners, where poor oppressed people were digging rich treasures for those called Christians, and heard them blaspheme the name of Christ, at which I was grieved, for his name to me was precious.[9]

In the midst of this shadowed and gloomy vision Woolman also heard a soft melodious voice as of an angel, saying, "John Woolman is dead." When he came to himself, and was informed by those around him that he was really John Woolman, he found himself repeating the verse of Scripture, "I am crucified with Christ, nevertheless I live; yet not I, but Christ liveth in me."[10] He then understood that what the angel had been announcing was the death of John Woolman's will. He was no longer to live for himself, but as a wholly dedicated servant of God to be "mixed in" with all humankind.

The Journal gives repeated evidence, however, that no matter how strong Woolman's concern was for issues of social and public justice, his central emphasis was upon personal and spiritual values. He believed and practiced the scriptural precept, "Keep your heart with all vigilance, for from it flow the springs of life" (Proverbs 4:23). In a pointed example of wise spiritual counsel, he admonishes himself and his fellow ministers:

Thou who sometimes travellest in the work of the ministry and art made very welcome by thy friends, seest many tokens of their satisfaction in having thee for their guest. It is good for thee to dwell deep, that thou mayest feel and understand the spirits of people. It is needful for us to take heed that their kindness . . . do not hinder us from the Lord's work.[11]

Yet *The Journal* is a book for all Christians, no matter what their church affiliation may be. A striking passage dated in the Quaker manner, "Fourth of fourth month, 1757," expresses the author's thoroughly ecumenical spirit:

I have been informed that Thomas à Kempis lived and died in the profession of the Roman Catholic religion; and, in reading his writings, I have believed him to be a man of a true Christian spirit, as fully so as many who died martyrs because they could not join with some superstitions in the Church. All true Christians are of the same spirit, but their gifts are diverse, Jesus Christ appointing to each one his peculiar office, agreeably to his infinite wisdom.[12]

John Woolman served God in his own generation. He was a voice crying in the wilderness of the colonial time. But his words—on almost every page—are startlingly pertinent today. People still fear to walk in the ways of God, the ways of honesty, unselfishness, truth, and love; instead, they seek to subject others to their will, or to outwit and take some advantage of them. Woolman's simple ways and guileless Christian practice many never become popular. But they bear their strong, quiet witness. And here and there are those who cannot resist, but instead rise up and follow in the same path of righteousness. They are the salt of the earth.

THE SETTING: 19th-century Denmark
THE BOOK: A profound philosopher, captured by Christ, summons his
readers to spiritual reality and Christian cross-bearing

11

For Self-Examination

Søren Kierkegaard

Even though we are all baptized, every man may well need
to become a Christian in another sense.

The writings of Søren Kierkegaard concerning the spiritual life
differ sharply from those of other great devotional books in at least two
respects. In the first place, many of his earlier books deal only indirectly
with the problems of religious faith; and second, all his writing has
a strong element of irony, aimed at exposing the subtle sins and self-
deceptions of the human heart. Living in a nominally Christian land,
Kierkegaard came to see the Christianity around him as shallow and
hypocritical, a poor imitation of real Christianity. He was brought up in
the church and in the "Christian" philosophy of his time, but more and
more he turned against them in disillusionment, first denouncing them
with tongue and pen. In this struggle he finally gave his life. Broken in
body and spirit, he collapsed on the street in his native city, and a few
days later died at the age of forty-two.

Hundreds of passages in his devotional books bear witness that
few writers can speak more gently to the burdened heart than Søren

Kierkegaard. But he saw with uncompromising clarity that if there is to be inward healing, there must first be honest heart searching and penitence. The title of his book *For Self-Examination* is significant: before we can come to God, we must first "come to ourselves."

Kierkegaard's tragic life affected all his writing, even more than for most authors. Therefore, some knowledge of his life can help us to understand his message. He was born in Copenhagen on May 5, 1813, the youngest of seven children. His parents moved to the city from Jutland some years later, and his father had become so successful as a wool merchant that he was able to retire at the age of forty. He was fifty-five when Søren was born, and they had a strong and enduring relationship. But Michael Pedersen Kierkegaard's spirit was one of deep melancholy. Despite his business success and his fine community standing, he could not escape the burden of some deeply hidden secrets in his past. Long afterward, Søren learned that one day during his years of poverty as a boy on the Jutland heath, his father had climbed up a little hill, clenched his fist, looked up to heaven, and cursed God. Afterward, he felt that a curse rested upon him and his family.

So Søren Kierkegaard's life was clouded from the very beginning. Like his father, he too became a prisoner of melancholy. His whole life experience—the books he wrote, the struggles he endured, even his interpretation of the Christian life—all were related to and marked by a sense of the somberness, the suffering, the sorrow of life.

He began his studies at the University of Copenhagen at the age of seventeen, concentrating on literature, philosophy, and theology. His university years were a time of intellectual and spiritual struggle. The prevailing philosophical defenses of religion failed to answer his probing questions, and for a time he completely rejected the Christian faith. His moral convictions gave way, as well, and he lived a life of self-indulgence and dissipation. Breaking with his father, he moved away from home to a rented apartment. He squandered money on expensive food, drink, clothes, and friends—leaving his father to pay the bills. He traveled mile by mile to the far country. Later he called it "the road to perdition."

But the husks of sin and unbelief could not satisfy his soul, and the rationalistic philosophy prevailing at the university left his mind unconvinced. Then, at the age of twenty-five, partly influenced by the writings of German philosopher Johann Hamann and stirred by the loss of a close friend, he began to turn homeward again toward his childhood faith.

The outward expression of this is indicated in the record of a Copenhagen pastor that on "July 6, 1838, S. Kierkegaard came to confession and took communion."[1]

Kierkegaard does not call this experience his "conversion": to the end of his life he insisted that he was only "becoming" a Christian. But in an entry in his journal dated May 19, 1838, 10:30 A.M., he writes of the great joy that had come to him:

> There is such a thing as an indescribable joy which glows through us. . . . Not a joy over this or that, but full jubilation "with hearts and souls and voices": a joy which cools and refreshes like a breeze, a gust of the tradewind which blows from the Grove of Mamre to the eternal mansions.[2]

For a time after this, Kierkegaard considered seeking ordination to the ministry, but this was not to be. He continued his studies and completed his master's degree. Meanwhile, another overwhelming influence had come into his life. He met and fell in love with a young woman named Regina Olsen. Since she was was only fourteen years old at the time, he suppressed his affection for several years before beginning to court her. But already during that time the thought of her brought him inspiration, profound reason for living and working. They became engaged early in 1841.

But almost immediately thereafter, Kierkegaard began to feel that the engagement was a mistake. He saw himself as completely unfit for marriage (what all of his reasons were has been the subject of study and debate for more than 100 years), and despite Regina's deep love and the urgent counsel of her parents, he set about to create a situation that would lead her to break the engagement. His plan was successful; the engagement was broken off in 1843. This strange episode became the most far-reaching influence on the rest of Kierkegaard's life.

The broken engagement initiated twelve years of continual writing and publication. Books, large and small, poured from his pen. At first they were books chiefly of philosophy, which sought to analyze the meaning of human life at all levels, books that for more than a century have gained an ever-widening readership, books whose purpose was to show indirectly but convincingly that the essence of life is to *live*, not to think or talk about living.

After passing through another major spiritual crisis in 1848, which gave him renewed assurance of "being drawn near to God," Kierkegaard entered upon the second—and final—phase of his authorship. Now the themes in his writing became exclusively devotional, addressed not primarily to the mind but also to the heart and will.

Among these devotional books one of the most heart-searching is *For Self-Examination*, published in 1851, only four years before his death. Though written in simple language, *For Self-Examination* is a powerful example of Kierkegaard's lifelong insistence that the chief ingredient in the Christian religion is *life*, not words. A story from one of his earlier books vividly illustrates this point:

> It is said to have chanced in England that a traveller was attacked on the highway by a robber who had made himself unrecognizable by wearing a big wig. He falls upon the traveller, seizes him by the throat and shouts, "Your purse!" He gets the purse and keeps it, but the wig he throws away. A poor man comes along the same road, puts it on and arrives at the next town where the traveller has already denounced the crime. He is arrested, is (mistakenly) recognized by the traveller, who takes his oath that he is the man. By chance the robber is present in the courtroom, sees the misunderstanding, turns to the judge and says, "It seems to me that the traveller has regard rather to the wig than to the man."[3]

So it is in Christendom, says Kierkegaard. We pay attention to the outward appearance, not to inward reality. *For Self-Examination* consists of three sermons, on the texts for the fifth Sunday after Easter, Ascension Day, and Pentecost. In the first we are brought face to face with God, in the second with the Son, in the third with the Holy Spirit. The text of the first sermon is from James 1:23–24:

> If any one is a hearer of the word, and not a doer, he is like a man who observes his natural face in a mirror; for he observes himself, and goes away and at once forgets what he was like.

James is sometimes said to teach a "gospel of works." But Kierkegaard immediately launches into a denunciation, not of works, but of a false reliance upon God's grace:

There is always a worldliness that is desirous of having the name of being a Christian but wishes to become one at as cheap a price as possible.[4]

True faith, however, "is a turbulent thing. It is health, but it is stronger and more violent than the most burning fever."[5]

But how are we to become such real Christians—with a "turbulent" inner faith that also expresses itself in a true outward life of witness? The basic answer, says Kierkegaard, lies in a right use of the Word of God.

The first requirement is that you must not look at the mirror and inspect the mirror, but see yourself in the mirror.[6]

So much time and effort and learning have been expended in study about the Bible: Who were the authors? Are they reliable? Have they themselves seen what they write about? What about the countless different interpretations? If we permit ourselves to be taken up with all these questions—studying the mirror—we many never get around to seeing ourselves in the mirror.

Actually, says Kierkegaard, the Bible is to be treated like a love letter from a loved one. In the reading of any love letter, heart speaks to heart. So must it be with one's reading of the Bible. Even the learned professors must read it in this way—not simply study the mirror. "Be sure to remember that when you read God's Word learnedly, with a dictionary, etc., you are not reading God's Word."[7] "If you are not learned, do not envy the scholar. Rejoice that you can begin reading God's Word at once!"[8] And if there are obscure passages in the Bible, do not be concerned about that. "It is not the obscure passages that bind you, but those which you understand."[9] Kierkegaard has only scathing rebuke for mere "interpretation" of the Bible:

All this interpretation and interpretation and science and new science is produced on the solemn, grave principle that it is for rightly understanding God's Word. Look more closely and you will see that it is to defend itself against God's Word—in about the same way as a boy who puts one or more napkins in his trousers when he is to get a thrashing.[10]

A further fundamental requirement for seeing oneself in the mirror is to constantly say to oneself, "It is talking to me; I am the one it is speaking about."[11] As Nathan pressed home to David the accusing words "Thou art the man," so must we let God's Word press its message home to our hearts: Our hearts are deceptive. We do not want to face the truth. We do not dare to look in the mirror. It is more pleasant to study it. But if we dare to look in the mirror in our reading, then

> sometimes you will read a fear and trembling into your soul, and, by God's help, you will succeed in becoming a man, a personality. You will be saved from being this horrible nonentity into which we human beings—created in God's image—have been bewitched, an impersonal objective something.[12]

Finally, having read this, we must not forget what we looked like. Instead, we must go immediately and obey. Here, too, we are deceptive. We are tempted to be like the drunkard who thinks he will stop drinking tomorrow. But we must deal sternly with our deceptive hearts and obey now!

The text for the second sermon, on Ascension Day, is from the first chapter of Acts, and the theme is "Christ is the Way." Once more Kierkegaard strikes the keynote: in Christianity, words must be rooted in life. Christ is the way because his life exemplified what he taught. The way is narrow because Christ's life was "narrow" from the very beginning: He was born in poverty. As a child he was already persecuted by the rulers. As he grew older, the way was still narrow and difficult. He had no place to lay his head. And always he was surrounded by temptation, not only in the desert, but everywhere. The greatest temptation of all was to compromise, to say less about himself than was true, to lower the standards for his followers. And ever before him lay the shadow of the cross. He loved his people and served them; but he knew that his very work of love was playing a part in bringing him to the cross.

The way became narrower and narrower as it progressed—all the way to death. Little by little, it became clear that he must "cast fire upon the earth" (Luke 12:49). His life and teachings would divide people, brother from brother, mother from daughter—in all generations. This was the bitterest cup of all. Yet he had to drink it, for love's sake. Death inescapable. Judas. Gethsemane. Calvary. Forsaken by God and others.

The way was narrow, ever, ever narrower—to the end. Then came the ascension—but only then. It was glorious, eternally glorious, but only *after* death. And that death was self-chosen.

Christ was not one who aspired to wealth but had to be satisfied with poverty. He *chose* poverty. And all who would follow him must choose the narrow way. They must imitate Christ. They must be identified with him. How complete this identification is between Christ and the believer comes clear in Kierkegaard's description of what it means to pray in the name of Jesus:

> I cannot pray in the name of Jesus to have my own will; . . . the fact that the name of Jesus Christ comes at the beginning is not prayer in the name of Jesus; but it means to pray in such a manner that I dare name Jesus in it; that is to say, think of him, think of his holy will together with what I am praying for; . . . It means . . . Jesus assumes the responsibility and all the consequences, he steps forward for us, steps into the place of the person praying.[13]

Sometimes we may be tempted to doubt the reality of the ascension, to doubt that Christ is really the victor who has overcome death. So it was for the apostles. What they suffered in following Christ purged them of every doubt. The proof of Christianity is not in argument but in the experience of following Christ. We are like the ten lepers: "as they went, they were cleansed."[14]

> And you, my listener, what do you do? Do you doubt the Ascension? If so, then do as I do. Say to yourself, "Well, this doubt is nothing to fuss about. I know very well where and how it came—from this, that I must have been careful of myself in regard to *imitating*, that my life is not exerted enough in this direction, that I have too easy a life, that I spare myself the risks which are bound up with witnessing for the truth and against untruth."[15]

Kierkegaard's final assertion concerning the ascension is simple and strong: when one suffers because one does good, because one is right, because one is loving—when it is for a good cause that one lives forsaken, persecuted, mocked, impoverished then one will not doubt his or her ascension, for one will need it![16]

In the third sermon, Pentecost Day, the day of the Holy Spirit, Kierkegaard begins ironically by saying that of course we believe in "the spirit of the age," "the world-spirit," "the human spirit"—all these are commonly accepted and are often casually referred to in conversation.[17] But when we are asked to speak of the Holy Spirit, we hesitate. And perhaps it is right we should, for "one cannot talk about there being a Holy Spirit and believing in a Holy Spirit without binding oneself by one's words."[18] To speak of the Holy Spirit seems to put us in touch with a world that lays solemn claim upon us. Pentecost is a day of deep and powerful earnestness.

Christianity, it is true, issues a universal invitation to life. And people eagerly cling to the life instinct. "Bring us life!" we cry. But Kierkegaard, the lookout on the walls of spiritual reality, sternly interposes:

> The life-giving in the Spirit is not a direct heightening of the natural life in a man, a spontaneous continuation in direct connection with the natural life—blasphemy! How dreadful to take Christianity in vain this way. . . . No, it is a new life, literally a new life—for mark this well, death goes between. . . . You must die, and the life-giving Spirit is the very one which kills you![19]

The apostles and the first church had to turn their backs on all the world; they had to die to every human confidence and human hope. After the cross—Christ's cross and their cross—came Pentecost. And so it must be with us. And this dying must be a matter of free personal choice, personal renunciation. At this point, Kierkegaard draws upon his own bitter experience in renouncing his betrothed and describes the lover's agony in freely choosing to give up his beloved:

> To be obliged to deprive oneself of the one he yearns for and now possesses—that is to wound selfishness at the root, as in the case of Abraham when God demanded that Abraham himself—how dreadful—with his own hand—horror and madness!—offer Isaac.[20]

To freely give up, renounce, wholly surrender—this is what God requires. Then Pentecost can come. Christianity inevitably involves the suffering of being delivered from selfishness. There is no escape, no alternative. To live we must die.

But then comes the life-giving Spirit, who can pour out upon us the rich gifts of faith and hope and love—not the faith and hope and love that are the natural attributes of human life, but the faith and hope and love flowing from the new life in the Spirit. Only these can in truth overcome and win the victory over the world. When the apostles had "died," when they had had

> the dreadful experience that love is not loved, that it is hated, ridiculed, spit on, crucified in the world, and crucified while justice in the judgment seat calmly washes its hand and while the people voice clamors for the robber, . . . by loving God they united themselves, so to speak, with God to love this world.[21]

Such is the mystery, the transforming mystery of Christian love—the mystery of the Spirit, the victorious mystery of Pentecost. With a beautiful story, Kierkegaard illustrates once more the truth that he never tires of reiterating: that the Christian life must be one of earnest discipline—but to live under the discipline of the Holy Spirit is to know life at its highest and best:

> Once upon a time there was a rich man who brought from abroad, at an exorbitant price, a team of faultless and excellent horses which he wanted for his own pleasure and the pleasure of driving them himself.

> A year or two passed by. If anyone who had known these horses in earlier days now saw them driven by their owner, he would not be able to recognize them. Their eyes had become dull and drowsy; their pace had no carriage and consistency. They could bear nothing; they could endure nothing. . . . Moreover, they had acquired all sorts of quirks and bad habits. Although they of course got food in abundance, they grew thinner day by day.

> The rich man called in the king's coachman. He drove them for one month. At the end of the period there was no team of horses in the whole land which carried their heads so proudly, whose eyes were so fiery, whose pace was so beautiful. . . . How did this happen? The owner, who was no coachman and merely played the coachman, drove the horses according to the horses' conception of how they should be driven.

The royal coachman drove them according to a coachman's conception of driving.[22]

Having given this stern challenge to all who would live the Spirit-filled and Spirit-controlled life, Kierkegaard closes the book with this gentle and moving prayer:

> O Holy Spirit, we pray for ourselves and for all men—Holy Spirit, Thou who givest life. Here there is no want of capabilities, of culture, of wisdom—rather there is too much of it. But what is wanted is that Thou shouldst take away that which exists for our ruin, take power from us in order to give us life. No doubt, when Thou dost take power from a man in order to become a power in him, it does not happen without a shudder, like the shudder of death. But if even animal creatures later came to understand how good it was for them that the royal coachman took the reins, though at first they surely were struck with terror and their minds rebelled in vain, should a human being then not quickly come to understand what a blessing it is for man that Thou dost take away the power and give life![23]

THE SETTING: 19th-century Orthodox Russia
THE BOOK: The experience of a "wanderer for Christ" who found the secret
of prayer without ceasing

12

The Way of a Pilgrim

Anonymous

*The calling upon the name of Jesus gladdened my way.
. . . And that is how I go about now, and ceaselessly
repeat the Prayer of Jesus, which is more precious
to me than anything in the world.*

A tragic break between the Christian churches of the East and West occurred in the year 1054. For more than 900 years, therefore, there was no official contact between these two great divisions of Christendom, the Orthodox East and the Roman Catholic West, each regarding itself as the only true heir and representative of apostolic Christianity. The two churches went their separate ways, each developing a distinguishable theology, liturgy, architecture, and piety. In the sixteenth century, the Western Church experienced a second great separation in the Protestant Reformation, and Christendom was fractured into three large divisions. Both Catholics and Protestants remained largely unfamiliar with the historical patterns, the writings, and the spirituality of Eastern Orthodoxy. Only within the past century has this gulf begun to be bridged, and both sides are slowly learning to know one another.

In an attempt to account for the differences in piety, it is sometimes said that Roman Catholicism takes St. Peter as its leader and stresses authority. Protestantism follows St. Paul and stresses individual experience, while Eastern Orthodoxy, following the spirit of St. John, stresses *sobornost*, or love and community in Christ. Such a classification is oversimplified, but at least it rightly points toward the "spirit" that is characteristic of the church in the East—an emphasis on love and humility and fellowship in Christ. In a number of Orthodox countries there existed for centuries a close alliance between state and church, sometimes actually involving the church in real bondage. But even then, beneath and beyond the outward structure and organizations, a warm life of spiritual love and fellowship often flourished in hundreds of monasteries, in the local congregations, and in the homes of the faithful.

One distinctive mark of Orthodox piety, especially in Russia, is *kenoticism*, referring to a self-emptying, and taking the lowest place— following the example of Christ, who "emptied himself" and took the form of a servant. For centuries Russian Christians have honored the ideal of poverty and humility as the highest form of Christlike life. All the great saints of Russia have been marked by the quality. Typical were Boris and Gleb, the royal brothers who permitted themselves to be killed rather than fight for the throne against their brother, and who became the first canonized Russian saints. But there were hundreds of others who lived lives of great holiness and humility, some of whose stories have never been written. For people in the United States, this remains an almost totally unexplored world of spiritual treasure.

Much of Orthodox spirituality has been centered in the monasteries. In the East there were no religious orders, such as there are in the Roman Catholic church; each community was self-governing, under the leadership of an abbot. In the monasteries, too, there were often *startsi*, elders of great spiritual insight, to whom people of all classes came for counsel. The figure of Father Zossima in Dostoyevsky's *The Brothers Karamazov* is an unforgettable example of a saintly Russian *starets*.

In old Russia another common religious pattern was "going on pilgrimage." There were thousands of pilgrims who left home and family and set forth to seek a deeper life with God. Some had a definite destination, such as Jerusalem or Kiev, but often the "wandering life" was adopted simply as a means of breaking off old contacts and reducing daily needs to a level where they could be met by incidental labor or by the charity of others. Among the pilgrims and in the monasteries there was a widespread use of the Jesus Prayer, a simple and beautiful form of devotion developed earlier among Greek-speaking monks in the Near East.

The Way of a Pilgrim gives us a delightful introduction to this spirituality as it was found in nineteenth-century Russia. This book by an anonymous writer was first published in Kazan in 1884. It purports to be a journal of a penniless pilgrim who travels among the Russian and Siberian villages and through the countryside, receiving food and lodging as it is given to him, conversing with many different types of people, always seeking the secret of a deeper, more continual life of prayer. The opening paragraph sets the scene:

> By the grace of God I am a Christian man, by my actions a great sinner, and by calling a homeless wanderer of the humblest birth who roams from place to place. My worldly goods are a knapsack with some dried bread in it on my back, and in my breastpocket a Bible. And that is all.[1]

The title, *The Way of a Pilgrim*, has a twofold meaning: On one hand, it tells about the way the pilgrim traveled and whom he met. But it also describes the particular way of prayer that he learned and practiced. The book captures the reader's attention at once—by its utter simplicity, by its depth of spiritual insight, and not least by the stream of various and interesting personalities the pilgrim encounters.

The pilgrim's earlier life was one of unhappiness. He was orphaned in childhood. When he was seven, he was crippled though the carelessness of his only brother. When they are grown, this brother steals the pilgrim's inheritance from his house. The pilgrim marries, but life is grim with hardship, and after but a few years his wife dies. In sorrow and loneliness he then gives away his few possessions and sets out on a wandering life, at first with no particular goal or motive.

One day in church he hears a sermon on the text, "Pray without ceasing" (1 Thessalonians 5:17). The words puzzle him. How can it be possible to pray at all times? Burdened by the question, he sets out to find a solution. His first inquiries bring wholly unsatisfactory answers, but at last he encounters a gentle starets who undertakes to teach him to pray the Jesus Prayer, that is, to repeat over and over again, either audibly or silently, "Lord Jesus Christ, Son of God, have mercy on me, a sinner."

By concentration and long practice, the pilgrim finds that this prayer becomes almost second nature to him. He can say it thousands of times a day without difficulty. After a period of time, he finds himself praying it even in his sleep.

To those of us who have had no experience with this prayer, it may at first seem mechanical and lacking in meaning. But such was not the experience of the pilgrim; rather, it brought him great joy. Here is how he describes the effect of the prayer upon him:

> Sometimes my heart would feel as though it were bubbling with joy; such lightness, freedom, and consolation were in it. Sometimes I felt a burning love for Jesus Christ and for all God's creatures. . . . . Sometimes that sense of a warm gladness in my heart spread throughout my whole being and I was deeply moved as the fact of the presence of God everywhere was brought home to me.[2]

He repeatedly assures us, too, that the Jesus Prayer is by no means only for monks, but also for anyone who is willing to learn. Once the pilgrim has learned this secret of joyous intensive prayer, he gladly shares it with anyone along his way who will listen to him. As he travels from village to village, the people he meets are many and varied—rich and poor, old and young, good citizens and lawbreakers. The pilgrim himself constantly learns from life; often, too, he becomes a teacher, especially by exemplifying a constant spirit of humble gratitude to both other people and God. He writes,

> During my wanderings . . . I happened to pass through a certain country town. My supply of dried bread had run very low, so I went to one of the houses to ask for some more. The householder said, "Thank God, you have come just at the right moment, my wife has only just taken the bread out of the oven, so there is a hot loaf for you. Remember me in your prayers." I thanked him and was putting the bread away in my knapsack, when his wife, who was looking on, said, "What a wretched state your knapsack is in, it is all worn out. I'll give you another instead." And she gave me a good strong one. . . . I rejoiced in spirit and thanked God for leading me, unworthy as I was, to such kindly folk. "Now," thought I, "without having to worry about food I shall be filled and content for a whole week. Bless the Lord, O my soul!"[3]

Often the pilgrim reports a conversation that is rich in both sound thinking and spiritual insight. In once such instance, he has been visiting with a young priest who has invited him to dinner. In response to a question, the priest sets forth this instructive method of meditation and prayer:

> To become a man of recollected interior life, you should take some one text or other of Holy Scripture and for as long a period as possible concentrate on that alone all your power of attention and meditation; then the light of understanding will be revealed to you. You must proceed the same way about prayer. If you want it to be pure, right, and enjoyable, you must choose some short prayer consisting of few but forcible words, and repeat it frequently and for a long time. Then you will find delight in prayer.[4]

People in the West are perhaps a bit prejudiced against such repetition in our prayers, but anyone who tries out these directions will find that they are indeed helpful and have the wisdom of long experience. But actually, the totality of prayer is much more inclusive than these simple practices. In one of the pilgrim's conversations, in a home where he is a guest, he reads to his host this quotation from one of Peter of Damascus:

> The Apostle says, "Pray without ceasing." That is, he teaches men to have the remembrance of God in all times and places and circumstances. If you are making something, you must call to mind the Creator of all things; if you see the light, remember the Giver of it. . . . If you put on your clothes, recall Whose gift they are and thank Him Who provides for your life. In short, let every action be a cause of your remembering and praising God, and lo! you will be praying without ceasing and therein your soul will always rejoice.[5]

On another occasion, when a fellow pilgrim expresses a strong aversion for the Jews, the starets with whom they are visiting rebukes him with a wisdom that gives a genuine Christian answer to anti-Semitism:

> You have no right, friend, to abuse and curse the Jews like this. God made them just as he made us. The disgust that you feel for them comes

from the fact that you are not grounded in the love of God and have no interior prayer as a security and therefore, no inward peace. The soul which is inwardly united to God becomes, in the greatness of its joy, like a good-natured, simple-hearted child, and now condemns no one, Greek, heathen, Jew, nor sinner.[6]

In an especially moving incident, the pilgrim is able to convince a deserter from the army who has also become a thief and a drunkard, to try the simple way of prayer and thereby to find his way back to God and a renewed joy in life. The transforming power of the Gospel is constantly in action through him.

Although the pilgrim has no automatic solution for the ills of human life, his direct and guileless application of the gospel to dozens of difficult situations gives an inspiring portrayal of the working of Russian piety. It is no doubt true, as the Orthodox scholar G. P. Fedotov has pointed out that "the author has not the intention of depicting life around him as it is, but that of selecting instructive examples of Christian virtue."[7] In other words, the piety described was by no means universal in old Russia. Nevertheless, the picture given is a true one.

In the last two sections of the book, the form of presentation changed from a narrative to dialogue. The pilgrim has encountered another interesting and earnest traveler, a professor, and together they go to visit the starets again to seek his counsel. The latter has other visitors too, and the group is led into an extended discussion of various aspects of the prayer life. Each of the speakers has his own characteristic approach: the professor is keen and searching in his questions; the *skhimnik* (a monk of advanced spiritual experience) is profound and wise in counsel; the hermit understands and explains the values of the solitary life; the starets is a gentle man of deep faith who presides graciously over the whole discussion. Together they form a group of people pursuing a topic of great importance, the whole discussion having an involved, Russian flavor. The learning revealed in some of the speeches indicates that this part of *The Way of a Pilgrim* cannot be the work of an uneducated person, though perhaps the background material on which it is based may have been a pilgrim journal.

The discussants take up again the question of what prayer actually is, and the answer given is clear and helpful:

Truly to pray is to direct the thought and the memory without relaxing, to the recollection of God, to walk in His divine Presence, to awaken oneself to His love by thinking about Him, and to link the name of God with one's breathing and the beating of one's heart. [The earnest seeker after God] is guided in all this by the invocation of the lips of the most Holy name of Jesus Christ, or by saying the Jesus Prayer at all times and in all places and during every occupation unceasingly.[8]

An especially difficult question regarding the necessity and value of intercessory prayer is pointedly raised by the professor and illuminated by the skhimnik. The explanation given is based upon the influence that one personality can have upon another. In prayer we bring to bear the finest, highest influences upon those for whom we pray. Clearly and convincingly, the skhimnik shows that we are by no means to *convince* God, but rather to work *with* God.

An equally perplexing question regarding the value of silences and solitude is most helpfully discussed by the hermit. Human service, he says, is not rendered only through direct personal contact; sometimes the greatest help is conveyed through the hidden service of love and intercession. The world is bound together, not only physically, but also spiritually. The hermit, the soul of solitude, adds to the spiritual riches of the whole world and renews the very springs of life. In the end, the hermit quotes an anonymous spiritual writer who even contends the following:

If the State were developed to the highest degree of education and morals, yet even then it would still be necessary to provide people for contemplation, in addition to the general activities of the citizen, in order to preserve the spirit of truth . . . to keep it for the generations to come and hand it on to posterity.[9]

The dialogue comes to an end as the pilgrim and the professor leave to set out again on their journey to a monastery in the far north, asking that the others pray for them on their way. Finally, the starets pronounces a beautiful scriptural benediction.

Not many people today would be drawn to adopt the outward lifestyle of the pilgrim, nor perhaps even to follow the forms of prayer and meditation recommended in his book. The contemporary United

States is far removed from nineteenth-century Russia. But the inner essence of the pilgrim's life is certainly worthy of our study and our pursuit: an earnest desire for spiritual instruction, a continuing hidden life of prayer, simplicity of life and honesty of speech, brotherliness and helpfulness toward all whom we meet, sincere participation in the life of the church, faith in divine guidance along life's way. These are priceless spiritual qualities that we all would do well to seek out and to cultivate. For all who desire to have a part in this noble quest, the pilgrim's ways and words can be a perennially inspiring guide.

13

Creative Prayer

E. Herman

There comes a moment when we realize that our work for God is a shoddy, futile business, unless it is backed at every point by the apostolate of prayer.

Spiritual classics have their origin in many places—in the scholar's study, in the monastery, and in prison. *Creative Prayer*, by Emily Herman, is the product of a modern Presbyterian manse and a journalist's office. Though not yet as well known as some of the older spiritual classics, it explores the same themes concerning the deeper life with God, analyzed and clarified by a singularly keen and dedicated mind. Together with her minister-husband, she served first in Constantinople, then in Australia, where she gained recognition as a journalist through a column she edited in *The Australian Christian World*. When E. Herman and her husband returned to London, she served on the staffs of several outstanding religious journals. Her writing soon becoming widely known for both its striking style and its penetrating spiritual insight.

Besides her journalistic work and her spiritual writing, E. Herman published two books in the field of philosophical religion. Thus both her life and her writing were constantly nourished and formed by serious intellectual discipline. She read widely in English, French, German, and Latin. Someone who knew her closely wrote in a tribute published after her death, "Hers was a mind of supreme and piercing ability, of keenest analytic and critical quality."[1]

Yet her life was by no means narrowly intellectual in its interests. She participated actively in the life of her church; she loved social life and conversation, where she could also exercise her sparkling wit; she was an avid and gifted letter writer. Her list of pastimes included "country rambles" and "folklore." But her interests and her activities alike were centered in the spiritual—and the spiritual was centered in Christ. In her later years she became a member of the Anglican church (taking Brigid as a new Christian name), but this was only a further step in the development of her essentially ecumenical outlook, so well expressed in one of her essays:

> The Way which is in Christ is no private way. It is the King's highway. . . . On it we meet the sweeping winds of divine purpose, and the details of doctrinal conviction and practical methods drops into their proper subordinate places.[2]

Throughout her books her teaching is not sectarian but totally Christian. So also was her life and character. Concerning the Anglo-Catholic period in E. Herman's life, Dr. Duncan Macgregor writes,

> The beautiful humility always characteristic of her was deeper than ever before. The unselfishness of her dealings, and her spirit of self-sacrifice also, became more notable. She practiced asceticism, caring nothing for comfort, and was not too careful even about health. She was filled with a great and burning passion for the Person of Christ, and gave herself with a full abandonment to the service of Christ and her fellows.[3]

E. Herman died on December 2, 1923, at the age of forty-eight. *Creative Prayer*, published in 1921, gives us the mature fruit of her thought. Since that time, it has won for itself a place among the classics of the spiritual life. In a number of key passages, the author speaks to us directly on the great themes with which she deals.

She begins with a discussion of what prayer really is. Prayer is not a half-magic way of achieving our own goals. Nor is it a method of putting ourselves 'into tune with the energies of the universe," as some modern writers have taught. It is not a form of begging or pleading. "Prayer in its essence is communion with God."[4] All of the beneficial results of prayer life flow from this central reality. E. Herman illustrates the transforming effect of prayer by a striking comparison with the effect of a human friendship:

> As we are initiated into the mystery of friendship, we know that our friend is not merely "another"; he speaks to us not from without but from the center of our being. He is in us and we in him. . . . No merely temperamental affinity can account for friendship at its highest potency. Deep down in the abysmal mystery of being was the thread spun that linked soul to soul. My friend creates me and recreates me. His love and trust purge me of sin by shame and contrition, his gentleness makes me great, his high expectations make all things possible to me. And what is true in a limited measure of human friendship is wholly true of man's communion with his Creator.[5]

Among the essential aspects of a true prayer life, E. Herman stresses the following: 1) the cultivation of silence, 2) full surrender to God, 3) spiritual discipline, and 4) inward transformation. Concerning the first of these she says the following:

> The saints were capable of spiritual silence simply because they had not contracted our modern habit of ceaseless talk in their ordinary life. Their days were days of silence, relieved by periods of conversation, while ours are a wilderness of talk with a rare oasis of silence.

> It is useless to imagine that one can pass at a bound from a daily round in which the lust of talk absorbs three-fourths of the soul's energy to a state of harmonious revealing stillness. The practice of silence must begin, not in the "quiet hour" or in the fellowship-meeting, but in the office and the home, the playing field and the Church.[6]

From a cultivation of true silence can come a tremendous sense of peace and power:

Everyone who knows anything about the interior life knows that there is indeed a moment in our communion with God in which the soul knows itself to be alone with Him in the world, and knows also that in that august aloneness lie peace and power. It was in his hours of solitary communion with the Father that Jesus heard the cry of the world's life and looked deep into its heart.[7]

This can also be our experience as well. Deep personal prayer is not an escape from the world, but rather it is a profound entering into the needs and sorrows (as well as the joys) of other people:

The solitary worshipper who really touches God, and touches him not with a merely self-regarding motive, but with a heart of love for all men and a tender fellow-feeling with human need and woe, is engaged in a more genuine act of fellowship than a thousand gregarious individuals who mistake external togetherness for vital unity.[8]

Concerning the full surrender to God, which is both the result of and the further preparation for prayer, E. Herman quotes the great French spiritual writer J. N. Grou:

To give heart and mind to God so that they are ours no longer; to do good without being conscious of it; to pray ceaselessly and without effort, as we breathe; to love without stopping to reflect upon our feelings; to go ever onward without pausing to measure our progress—such is the perfect forgetfulness of self which casts us on God, as a babe rests upon its mother's breast. It is not by great deeds, long prayers, or even heavy crosses that we may best give glory to God; self-will may taint all these, but total self-renunciation does in truth give Him all the glory.[9]

E. Herman's own words bear the same message, with the added clarifying emphasis that surrender is not a once-for-all experience but a lifelong process:

The central thing in prayer is not the garden of the soul, but the altar of dedication. If we can go to that altar with joy and singing, happy are we; but more blessed are those who ascend its steps in the nakedness of faith, giving all for all and asking nothing in return, save that the will of God may be fulfilled in them.[10]

And further:

The life of prayer is the life of conversion—a gradual, progressive turning from self to God. Potentially and ideally, that conversion is accomplished in the first genuine act of surrender, whereby the soul dissociates itself from sin and enters into a right relation with Eternal Love; actually it involves a lifetime of successive and growing complete acts of daily self-denial and daily integration into Christ, a yielding up of the self that it may be filled with the fullness of God, a losing of life that it may be found again in Him.[11]

A little later she continues:

It is at this point that the soul is drawn to the prayer of intercession. . . . Prayer is seen as an apostolate, a means of making God known to others.[12]

And then she goes on to a daring assertion, which inevitably reminds us of Martin Luther's words in *The Freedom of the Christian* about each of us being called to be a Christ for others. E. Herman says,

We feel that since Christ Himself wrought our salvation for others by a life of obedience even to the death of the Cross, so we, being joined to Him and living in union with Him, can offer our prayers, and the life behind our prayers, on behalf of others.[13]

Such a life of surrender, of oblation to God, inevitably involves discipline, both inward and outward. Nor is this only a hard and painful ordeal; rather it adds zest and meaning to our experience and even casts a strange hidden glory over life. In the light of this twofold aspect of all spiritual discipline, E. Herman boldly calls us to "go into the front lines":

There is among us an unhealthy cult of life which militates against the ideal of discipline. In our anxiety to lay due emphasis upon the positive, constructive character of Christianity, we have made a shibboleth of its doctrine of free, abundant, overflowing life, athrill with splendid vigor and indefeasible gladness. . . . We must at all costs recover the splendid spiritual courage which casts life behind its back, that puts self beneath its feet. That royal habit of soul may conceivably be created and sustained without daily discipline and mortification; but if so, we have no record of such an achievement in all the annals of sanctity.[14]

During a period of war many a man who had lived comfortably and at ease and found life a dreary, ineffectual business, suddenly discovers a well of joy and power in himself, once he endures the hard discipline of camp and fighting-line. And we may experience the same change in our spiritual life, if we would only discard our dilettante conception of freedom and go into the front lines with Christ[15]

E. Herman is clear, too, that sometimes and for some people the discipline requires also the renunciation of both life's luxuries and necessities:

The call to evangelical poverty in the specific sense is something entirely distinct from any social theory. It is the response of the loving heart to the demand of Christ to "sell all" and follow Him. . . . It is the vocation of those who offer themselves to God that they might express in their persons the poverty of Christ and so become living sacraments, as it were, of the Incarnation. Those who are thus called rejoice in sharing the common life of the poor. They do not frown on earthly possessions, or decry the good things of material life. They choose poverty, not because they think it meritorious or good in itself, but because they believe that by renouncing legitimate comfort and being poor with Christ, they are hastening the day when disabling poverty shall be wiped off the face of the earth, and all men shall share in God's good gifts. They are poor that they may make many rich.[16]

Those who walk with God along these stern and blessed ways will come to know the indescribable joys of being gradually transformed—or suddenly transformed anew—into the likeness of God. To experience even a part of these things is indeed to "behold as in a mirror the glory of the Lord" and to be "transformed into the same image from glory to glory." The beginning of life in God is but a beginning. There are always further steps to be taken as we go forward in the life of the Spirit. For although all the riches of Christ are given in the initial gift of faith, often it is only much later that they are fully received. E. Herman's description of this "further-going" experience is couched in language that seems to strain to put into human words what is really beyond words:

> Then, perhaps by a sudden sharp invasion of a new life . . . we become conscious of the birth of the Christ spirit within ourselves, and of our own birth into a new and wonderful world. . . . It is the world of which God is the center. We look upon Him, and our life is renewed. We are given a set of new values, a spiritual coinage other than that with which we have hitherto traded. Things that but a little while ago seemed desirable now appear as dross. . . . We discover untold beauties in God; we find in Christ secrets of final restitution that fill us with a deathless hope. Matter is seen to be the storehouse of unguessed spiritual treasure, a hiding-place of holy powers, a laboratory of Divine alchemy. Everywhere we see mysteries of healing and regeneration of individual transfiguration and world renewal that remained hidden while self was our center. . . . It is as though we had developed a new set of faculties of appreciation and distaste, pleasure and pain.[17]

And this is not by any means only a solitary experience of the soul's great joy in God. All its joys are shared, as it shares and bears also the sorrow of others.

> At the very threshold of a sharply individual experience, the soul that is truly submitted to God will realize its oneness with all men. It is not a question of cultivating the corporate feeling, as if it were something super-added to man's experience of Christ.

> God sees us not merely as individuals, but also in an ideal relation to our fellows; and as the love of God is shed abroad in our hearts, we shall freely and generously identify ourselves with the weakest and most wayward, bearing their burdens and taking them into the center of our prayers. . . . The soul in whose depth Christ is truly born covets no spiritual privileges that make for isolation, refusing to be made perfect without its fellows.[18]

Such are some of the wonders of the life of prayer, the life of ever-deepening communion with God, as E. Herman presents them. The quotations given here, though not brief, are still fragmentary; but they are representative. The whole book merits thoughtful, prayerful reading. And none of us needs to be discouraged if much of what she says is still beyond us. For all of us, whatever our present stage of spiritual growth, there are heights still to be scaled and valleys still to be traversed. And all of us need the shining vision ahead to stir our lagging steps.

Creative Prayer unfolds an ideal and a pattern of prayer that will both allure and guide very earnest reader on the way inward and upward. A final quotation recapitulates the teaching of the whole book:

> Prayer, in most cases, begins with personal petition. We ask benefits for ourselves and for those we love. Then we come to realize that the power of prayer lies not in the external benefit, or even in the mental and spiritual reinforcement, that comes to us through it, but in the communion with God. A new love takes possession of us, a new relationship transfigures life, a new world dawns upon our unsealed eyes. We know that communion with God does not only mean mastery over life, but that it is life itself. And as we humbly press closer to the heart of God and read a little of its secret it is gradually borne in upon us that it is only as we die for self-love that we shall be able to take our true place within the heart of love. We see that prayer is a long and arduous pilgrimage from self to God, not, indeed, the pilgrimage of those who imagine that God can be reached by human effort, but the progress of souls that have been redeemed by Christ, and now desire to be wholly found in Him.[19]

14

Prayer

O. Hallesby

*Prayer is the breath of the soul, by which we receive
Christ into our parched and withered hearts.*

Every great book of devotion is the expression and outflow of a
larger spiritual movement in which the author's life was nourished, and
without which the book could never have been written. This is true of
Prayer, by Professor Ole Hallesby of Norway. In it is distilled the essence
of the life-giving movements for religious renewal that stirred in
Scandinavia during the nineteenth century. It was written less than a
century ago, but its roots go back at least 200 years.

The Lutheran Reformation of the sixteenth century is one of the
major landmarks in the history of Western Christendom. Luther's attack
upon ecclesiastical corruption and his challenge to the external authority
of the papacy kindled flames of reform and spread swiftly, and within a
generation much of northern Europe had broken away from Rome.
"Justification by faith" and "the freedom of the Christian" became the
great watchwords and the controlling vision. But the victory of that evangelical vision among the masses of the people came only after centuries of

struggle. The slowness of the process can be seen clearly in the Scandinavian nations, which became Lutheran before the sixteenth century was over. But the churches came under the sponsorship and control of the governments, which often had more concern for outward form and organization than for the realities of spiritual life. Reading of the life of the churches and pastors in these countries during the seventeenth and eighteenth centuries can be a very disillusioning experience. The rites and records required by the state, and orthodoxy of doctrine, with little relation to the life of the people, seem to have been matters of chief importance to the clergy.

But in the late seventeenth and eighteenth centuries in Lutheran Germany there arose a movement for spiritual renewal, which was to have far-reaching influence within Protestantism. It came to be called "Pietism"—a name soon both beloved and derided. Like every great movement, it became the cause of division. The outstanding leader (who might be considered the founder) of the Pietist movement was Philip Jacob Spener, a pastor in Frankfort, Germany. Its basic principles were outlined in his famous book, *Pia Desideria* (or *Pious Goals*), published in 1675. The program Spener advocated emphasized six points. Read today, they seem not at all radical, but they really proposed a deep spiritual revolution in church life at that time. The six proposals were as follows: 1) more extensive use of the Scriptures; 2) exercise of the priesthood of believers; 3) more stress on practice, in contrast to knowledge, of Christianity; 4) conducting religious controversies in a spirit of love, penitence, and prayerfulness; 5) reforming schools and universities, with more emphasis on spiritual life; and 6) preaching for the purpose of edification.

Later, among the followers of Spener, small group meetings for united prayer, Bible study, and mutual edification came to have an important place among their activities, and this together with other aspects of their program often became a troublesome source of controversy within the church. Pietism was bitterly opposed and denounced, but it continued to spread. Sometimes, no doubt, it fostered undesirable practices, such as false legalism, the view that the true Christian life is expressed only in following external rules and standards. But essentially its goal was both noble and necessary: the promotion and nurturing of a deeply personal Christian faith and life.

The movement of spiritual awakening in the Scandinavian countries during the eighteenth and nineteenth centuries was not always directly traceable to pietist influences from Germany, but both the spirit and the aims, as well as the methods of working, were similar. In Sweden the leading publication of the movement was called *The Pietist*. In each country there arose strong spiritual leaders whose voices were heard and echoed throughout the nation. C. O. Rosenius in Sweden, Paavo Ruotsalainen in Finland, Vilhem Beck in Denmark, and Hans Nielsen Hauge in Norway were the most widely recognized of these leaders. They and their followers proclaimed essentially the same message: Christianity is life. It is not merely a doctrine or a form of church practice; it is new life in Christ. It summons people to repentance and personal faith, and to a lifestyle transformed from within.

The story of peasant preacher Hauge's spiritual awakening has been told and retold hundreds of times in prayer houses throughout Norway. The time was April 5, 1796, when Hauge was twenty-five years old, and the place was his father's farm in Tune, in southern Norway. Though nurtured in a pious home and a faithful attendant at the parish church, Hauge had long been troubled by religious doubts and questions. Now on this day, as he was working in the field, he began to sing the familiar hymn beginning with these words:

> Jesus, for Thee and Thy blessed communion
> Longing possesses my heart and my mind;
> Break down all barriers that hinder our union
> Draw me to Thee, O Redeemer most kind.[1]

As he was singing the stanzas of this hymn, suddenly he found his heart set free from every burden and filled with great joy. He has described the experience in these words:

> My heart was so uplifted to God that I don't know nor can express what took place in my soul. As soon as my understanding returned, I regretted that I hadn't served the loving and all-gracious God; now I felt that no worldly thing was of importance. It was a glory which no tongue can explain; my soul felt something supernatural, divine, and blessed. . . . I had a completely transformed mind, a sorrow over all sins, a burning desire that others should share the same grace.[2]

127

That very evening Hauge began witnessing to his new-found faith, first of all to his two sisters. Soon afterward he was speaking boldly in public. Many of his listeners were immediately brought under conviction of sin and their hearts turned to God. Students of Hauge's life-transforming experience have used various terms to describe it, such as conversion, awakening, spiritual breakthrough, rebirth. The important fact, however, is that what happened to him was decisive: he was set free, he knew himself to be a new person, and the reality of such a thoroughgoing change became the central emphasis in his preaching. Thus Hauge's experience set a kind of basic pattern for thousands of his disciples and followers. There is a direct line of spiritual descent from the reborn life of Hans Nielsen Hauge to the liberated life of fellowship with God portrayed in Ole Hallesby's *Prayer*.

Within but a few months after his experience, Hauge initiated a vigorous nationwide crusade of preaching and personal witness. Others joined him, and before long the movement became so threatening to the church authorities that Hauge was arrested and imprisoned. He came to spend many hard years in prison, which severely impaired his health. But he was still active in prison, with both his tongue and his pen.

Haugeanism struck strong roots, and in various forms has continued until this day as a strong spiritual force. As a result, there have been two dominant types of spirituality in Norway since then: one ecclesiastical, liturgical, and scholarly; the other informal, intensely personal, and evangelistic—in a word, *Haugean*.

During the first half of the twentieth century, the most powerful and popular representative of Haugean Christianity in Norway was Professor Ole Hallesby—theologian, evangelist, controversial leader, prolific author. Like Hauge, Hallesby, after years of unrest and spiritual searching, passed through a personal crisis that changed him from a religious "liberal" to an ardent believer. After completing his studies, he became a professor at the Independent Theological Faculty in Oslo, where he carried out a life-long work of teaching, writing, and preaching. For an entire generation he was the acknowledged leader of "conservative Christianity" in Norway.

Concerning his book *Prayer*, Hallesby confessed, "I have had more of a desire to write this book than possibly any other that I have written. And yet I have been more afraid of this one than any other."[3] He seemed to sense that he was dealing with the heart of Christian life. The little book, though written by a learned theologian, represents Scandinavian lay Christianity at its best. It is unpretentious in both style and content. But like the great devotional classics of every age, it deals with essentials. Simply and directly, it speaks to the awakened heart. In Scandinavia and North America, it has remained popular for seventy years.

As we begin to read *Prayer*, we immediately sense that here is a book that concerns itself above all with the individual believer. Little attention is given to the church as a worldwide community, even less to matters for church order or organization, none at all to questions of social policy or missionary strategy. True, there is a world-circling fellowship of prayer that is recognized and advocated, but it is not the main concern of this book. If we think of Baron von Hügel's famous definition of the three elements of religion as being the intellectual, the institutional, and the mystical, we would have to say that *Prayer* deals almost exclusively with the mystical element, the realm of the soul when the closet door has been shut, and we are alone with God.

Prayer begins with Christ's words in the third chapter of Revelation: "Behold, I stand at the door and knock: if any man hear my voice and open the door I will come in to him, and will sup with him, and he with me" (Revelation 3:20). No passage in the whole Bible, says the author, throws more light on prayer than this one. For it shows that it is not we, but God, who initiates prayer. "Before they call, I will answer," says the prophet (Isaiah 65:24). Prayer is not a matter of following any complicated or well thought-out program. It does not depend on human effort or exertion, but simply on our willingness to "open the door."

Paradoxical as it may seem, effectiveness in prayer grows out of a sense of helplessness on our part. Prayer is the breath of the soul. As the air surrounds our bodies on every side, so the grace and blessing of God encompass us, ready to enter every receptive heart. The Israelites bitten by serpents in the wilderness needed but to look, and there was healing. When sinners acknowledge their own helplessness, this very fact creates in them the humble, broken heart to which the Lord can truly minister:

> Helplessness is the decisive factor, not only in our prayer life, but in our whole relationship to God. As long as we are conscious of our helplessness, . . . we will expect nothing of ourselves and therefore bring all our difficulties and hindrances to God in prayer.[4]

Only after such a very strong emphasis upon our dependence and helplessness does Professor Hallesby go on to point out the other crucial element in prayer, namely *faith*. And this too he defines with disarming simplicity. Faith is not a state of mind or heart that we must "work up," as it were. Rather, it is simply coming to God in our need:

> You have more faith than you think you have. You have faith enough to pray; you have faith enough to believe that you will be heard.[5]

> I need not exert myself and try to force myself to believe or try to chase doubt out of my heart. Both are equally useless. . . . [I need] only to tell Jesus how weak my faith is. I have let Jesus into my heart, and he will fulfill my heart's desire.[6]

Against this fundamental background of prayer as an intensely personal relationship between the soul and God, Hallesby goes on to discuss the various aspects of the prayer life, its problems and its power, its struggles, its defeats, and its victories. Important sections of the book are concerned with prayer as work, as the instrument of our cooperation with God for his kingdom:

> Whenever we touch His almighty arm, some of his omnipotence streams in upon us, into our souls and into our bodies. And not only that, but, through us, it streams to others. . . . This power is entirely independent of time and space. . . . Here is an example of wireless transmission of power, which transcends the dreams of the boldest inventor.[7]

The vital work of intercession should be carried on not only for the great masses and movements of humankind, and for the church both at home and abroad, but it should also be directed on behalf of certain definite individuals. "Ask the Spirit of prayer," says Dr. Hallesby, "to assign to you the individuals for whom you should pray."[8]

> The work of praying is prerequisite to all other work in the kingdom of God, for the simple reason that it is by prayer that we couple the powers of heaven to our helplessness . . . the powers which can capture strongholds and make the impossible possible.[9]

Such a work of intercession needs and deserves careful planning and an ordered program for the prayer chamber. For most of us this can be helped by keeping a "prayer list." Hallesby speaks slightingly of most printed prayer books, but he highly commends personally written prayer books. And he recognizes that occasional lapses of memory or practice do not by any means invalidate the prayer program. He discusses at length, and evidently on the basis of personal experience, what a struggle it can be to enter regularly into the work of prayer. Satan is ever at hand to tempt and to disturb us. But victory is possible, where "the peace of God guards our hearts."[10] Intense activity, far-soaring thought, and well-formulated sentences are not at all necessary in prayer. The most important thing is just to be in the divine presence. There our own hearts are searched and cleansed and healed. And through us there can flow a healing stream to others.

Other problems of the prayer life are also effectively dealt with in the book: the relationship between obedience and prayer, the meaning of unanswered prayer, the place of fasting in prayer life, prayer and physical healing, the relationship between intercessory prayer and the divine omnipotence, the prayers of the unconcerted. In each instance the teaching is uncomplicated, clear, and convincing. The whole Christian life, and the prayer life, are presented in the spirit of Christ's words: "Unless you turn and become like children, you will never enter the kingdom of heaven" (Matthew 18:3). This high commendation of simplicity will be an offense to some readers. But again and again, beneath the unadorned and childlike words lie hidden treasures of great wisdom.

Appropriately, the final chapter deals with the work of the Holy Spirit, who is both the source and the sustainer of a true life of prayer. The Holy Spirit must be the companion and teacher of all who walk with Christ. And Christ has assured us that the Father will give the Spirit, the best of all gifts, to everyone who prays for the Spirit's coming. Then in truth we shall be girded for the work of God among us:

Such childlike petitions for the Spirit of prayer will little by little bring about the change in our prayer life which we hardly thought possible. Without noticing it ourselves, prayer will become the great unifying factor in our distracted and busy lives. . . . A longing to talk with God about everything will arise. Everything we see and hear in connection with our dear ones, our friends, our enemies, . . . temporal and spiritual affairs, small things and great, the hard and the easy, all the observations and experiences which fill and shape our daily lives, will naturally and readily begin to take the form of prayer. . . . The Spirit of prayer makes us so intimate with God that we scarcely pass through an experience before we speak to Him about it.[11]

And the angels on the prayer ladder raised to heaven go both up and down. Hallesby uses a different figure to convey the same truth:

The longer you live this kind of life, the more answers to prayer you will experience. As white snowflakes falling quietly and thickly on a winter day, answers to prayer will settle down upon you every step you take, even to your dying day. . . . The shower of answers to prayer will continue to your dying hour, nor will it cease then.[12]

The heritage of pietism developed significantly in the "awakening" movements in nineteenth-century Scandinavia, where the message was proclaimed clear and strong: Christianity is to be personally experienced, and the individual set free into a trustful, responsible fellowship with God. It is this message that is presupposed on every page of Hallesby's *Prayer*. For only a justified, liberated heart can experience intimate, childlike prayer life such as he describes. It is in this sense that *Prayer* is a "pietistic" book.

This type of lay Christianity has often been despised by the worldly-wise, at times also by the church. And it does have its weaknesses, such as a certain narrowness of outlook and frequently a lack of stress upon the worldwide Christian community. But in spite of these weaknesses, few spiritual lighthouses of Christendom are more dependable guides than lives of evangelical prayer.

At the same time, it is important to remember that other concepts of the prayer life are by no means on the lower level. Christians of widely varying practices and beliefs have known and written of the blessedness of the "interior castle," as St. Teresa described. The house of prayer has many mansions. The subtle self-analysis of St. Augustine and the prophetic social vision of John Woolman have their place as truly as Dr. Hallesby's uncomplicated language of the heart. In the church there is room for both activist and pietist, for both church leaders and church visitors, to kneel together.

15

The School of Charity

Evelyn Underhill

The Christian Creed is a handlist of the soul's essential requirements; the iron ration of truths, the knowledge of mighty realities, which rightly used is sufficient to feed and safeguard our supernatural life throughout its course.

Beginning to read Evelyn Underhill's *The School of Charity* is like rounding a curve on a mountain drive and suddenly coming upon a breathtaking view of far-stretching valleys and mountain heights. For this volume of meditations on the Nicene Creed, by one of the truly great religious writers of the twentieth century, combines a remarkable depth of thought, beauty of style, and sweeping spiritual perspective. To some it may at first seem like difficult reading, but if it is read thoughtfully and in not too large segments at a time, it will yield rewarding spiritual insight. For, in a sense, *The School of Charity* may be said to resemble *The Confessions* of St. Augustine—an almost inexhaustible source of both Scripture-grounded instruction and spiritual inspiration.

As in the case of many other spiritual classics, *The School of Charity* is a fruit of the life and experience of its author. The long road she traveled from doubt to faith is reflected again and again in her treatment of many difficult questions, which beset Christian thought in our time. To gain some knowledge of Evelyn Underhill's life is therefore perhaps the best preparation for sharing her high vision of the life in Christ.

Born in 1875, Evelyn Underhill was the daughter of a distinguished London barrister. Her childhood home was thoroughly secularized. (She described it in the terse sentence, "I wasn't brought up to religion.")[1] At home, however, she absorbed fundamental moral ideals, so that even as a young girl she made a long list of her faults and shortcomings. But it was only after many years of serious thought and a brilliant educational career at King's College in London that she gradually came to believe in God and the Christian faith. Years of earnest quest and discipline were spent under the tutelage of the greatest thinkers and the greatest saints of the Christian past. She discovered many of these writers early on, and their teachings were slowly absorbed into her experience and her writing.

It was through her 1911 book, *Mysticism*, that she achieved recognition as one of the outstanding religious writers of her time. As her outlook broadened over the years, she wrote in many fields, including fiction, theology, philosophy, education, poetry, and letters of spiritual counsel. All of these reflected and recorded her deepening development in thought and life. In *Mysticism*, her convictions seem not yet to be fully Christ-centered. But about the time of its publication, she came to know a great teacher and friend, the eminent Roman Catholic theologian Baron Friedrich von Hügel, whose influence would be decisive in her life from then on. She herself never became a Catholic, but von Hügel's teachings remained a guiding star for her even after his death in 1925.

Revealing how long were the years of her spiritual quest, as late as 1927 she writes of herself,

> Until about five years ago I never had *any* personal experience of our Lord. . . . I was a convinced Theocentric. . . . I had, from time to time, what seemed to be vivid experiences of God, from the time of my

conversion from agnosticism (about 20 years ago now). . . . I went to the
Baron. . . . Somehow by his prayers or something he *compelled* me to
experience Christ. . . . The New Testament, which once I couldn't make
much of, or meditate on, now seems full of things I never noticed.[2]

The School of Charity, written a few years later, shows how far her
convictions had by that time been transformed. Evelyn Underhill was a
scholar of the highest order. Her books deal profoundly with the whole
field of Christian spirituality—its intellectual basis, its liturgical expression, its history in the lives of the saints, its daily application in present
experience. Her scholarly achievement was given notable recognition by
her being awarded an honorary Doctorate in Divinity by Kings College.
Yet as she pursued these ways of far-ranging study and inward discipline, her personal life was not isolated from ordinary human experience. She loved the country—the trees, the flowers, and the birds. She
traveled often. After her marriage in 1907, she kept her evenings, aside
from special duties, for her husband and home; she cultivated close personal friendships; for a long period she spent two afternoons a week
among the poor in the slums and near-slums of London. No one believed
more completely in the principle of incarnation than she—the spirit
must clothe itself with flesh in every area of life. Concerning the total
impact of Underhill's life, her devoted friend and the editor of her
Letters, Charles Williams, wrote the following:

> Her vocation was rather to be . . . in the end, a light. The light might,
> and certainly did, illuminate and guide, but first it merely shone.[3]

The light that shines through *The School of Charity* is, above all, that
of a beautiful life found by Christ after long seeking, and then lived out
in him. In harmony with the author's own experience of a parallel development of her inner life and her full acceptance of a Christ-centered
faith, *The School of Charity* directs us to both an inward pilgrimage of
prayer and discipleship and an ever-deepening faith, centered in the
incarnate Christ.

At the very heart of the Christian faith is the doctrine that the Word
became flesh. But this is not an isolated article in the creed; it is integral
with our whole faith in the triune God, indeed with our view of all
reality. The vision of God, however, too splendid for our human eyes,

135

can truly come to us only as reflected in the humility of the Incarnate One and only as we see it from "within"—with eyes and hearts that have been cleansed by prayer. Underhill uses a familiar example, giving it a beautiful twofold interpretation:

> It sometimes happens that one goes to see a cathedral which is famous for the splendor of its glass; only to discover that, seen outside, the windows give us no hint whatever of that which awaits us within. They all look alike; dull, thick, and grubby. . . . Then we open the door and go inside . . . and at once we are surrounded by a radiance, a beauty, that lie beyond the fringe of speech. The universal Light of God in which we live and move, and yet which in its reality always escapes us, pours through those windows . . . and shows us things of which we never dreamed before.

> In the same way, the deep mysteries of the Being of God . . . cannot be seen by us, until they have passed through a human medium, a human life. Nor can that life, and all that it means as a revelation of God, his eternal truth and beauty, be realized by us from the outside. . . . It is only within the place of prayer, recollection, worship and love . . . that we can cleanse our vision . . . and fully and truly receive the revelation of Reality which is made to us in Christ. . . .

> For here, a Light we can bear to look at . . . comes to us from a Light we cannot bear to look at even whilst we worship it. . . . What we see is not very sensational. . . . First we see a baby, and a long hidden growth; and then the unmeasured outpouring and self spending of an other-worldly love and mercy; teaching, healing, rescuing and transforming, but never trying to get anything for itself; . . . consummated at last in the most generous and lonely of deaths, issuing in a victory which has given life ever since to men's souls.[4]

The Incarnation, both as the perfect revelation of the heart of God and as the perfect pattern for every Christ-centered human life, continues to unfold throughout the whole earthly life of our Lord:

> We see the new life growing in secret. . . . We see the child in the carpenter's workshop. He does not go outside the frame of the homely

life in which he appeared. It did quite well for him, and will do quite well for us. There is no need for peculiar conditions in order to grow in the spiritual life. . . . The third-rate little town among the hills . . . reproves us when we begin to fuss about our opportunities and our scope. And this quality of quietness, ordinariness, simplicity, with which the saving action of God enters history, endures from the beginning to the end.[5]

Nor was this revelation of Incarnate Love among the routine scenes of human life broken off even by the shattering experience of the Passion and the Cross. After the Easter triumph it continued on the same level, giving of itself amidst common and everyday surroundings, reaffirming the pattern for the lives of all who would follow in his steps:

The [resurrected glory] of the Divine Humanity is not shown in the Temple and the Synagogue. He seeks out his nervous followers within the arena of ordinary life, meets them behind the locked doors of the Upper Room, waits for them in the early morning by the lakeside, walks with them on the country road, and suddenly discloses himself in the breaking of bread. The characters of the old life which are carried through into this new and glorified life are just those which express a homely and cherishing love.[6]

And so it must be, says Evelyn Underhill, in every true Christian life:

The real mark of spiritual triumph—the possession of that more love-ly, more abundant life which we discern in moments of deep prayer—is not an abstraction from this world, but a return to it; a willing use of its condition as material for the expression of love. There is nothing high-minded about Christian holiness. It is most at home in the slum, the street, the hospital ward. . . . A little water, some fragments of bread, and a chalice of wine are enough to close the gap between two worlds, and give the soul and senses a trembling contact with the Eternal Charity. By means of these its creatures, that touch still cleanses, and that hand still feeds.[7]

In addition to its being so intimately an outgrowth of the author's own life experience, there are three other elements in the content of

The School of Charity that contribute to its uniquely helpful character as a spiritual guide: 1) its solid basis in the Christian creed; 2) its constant reference to the great devotional writers of the past; and 3) its complete church-centeredness.

For Evelyn Underhill, the entire Nicene Creed is both a treasury of biblical truth and a "handlist of the soul's essential requirements." The most basic equipment for the Christian's journey through life, she says, is not a set of rules or methods, but rather a deepened understanding of the foundation of his faith. She calls upon her readers, therefore, as a salutary Lenten exercise (the book was originally written for Lent) to make a careful reexamination of the various elements in that equipment:

> Lent is a good moment for such spiritual stocktaking; a pause, a retreat from life's busy surface to its solemn deeps. There we can consider our possessions; and discriminate between the necessary stores which have been issued to us, and must be treasured and kept in good order, and the odds and ends which we have accumulated for ourselves.[8]

To undertake such a spiritual stocktaking, to ask yourself what you really believe on this or that issue, requires courage. But it is a very useful exercise, and anyone who has tried it can testify to its bracing effect on the soul. To examine, under Evelyn Underhill's guidance, the enduring realities of revelation and experience that sustain our convictions concerning the spiritual world in which we live, is indeed to be led anew into paths of deepened faith and righteousness.

Securely built upon the Christian creed, *The School of Charity* also draws widely upon the riches of other devotional writings from all the churches, East and West, Protestant, Catholic, and Orthodox. Evelyn Underhill was at home in all the Christian traditions and learned freely and gratefully from them all. Her writings are replete with references to the lives and the teachings of the saintly men and women of other generations, calling us to heed their words and follow in their footsteps:

> The Power that desires to fill and use us, is the Power that filled and used Paul and Augustine, Benedict, Bruno and Bernard, Francis of Assisi and Catherine of Siena, Fox and Wesley, . . . that went to the ends of the earth with Francis Xavier and Henry Martyn, or transformed a narrow sphere

in Father Wainwright and the Cure d'Ars. . . . We are "called to be saints"—self-emptied vessels of the Holy—not for our own sake but for the sake of the world. . . . In the world of spirit, that which is done by one is done by all since the real actor is the Charity of God.[9]

For Evelyn Underhill, the communion of saints was a basic reality undergirding the whole Christian experience. She herself lived in the truth proclaimed in her words, "Entering the mighty current of living charity, means entering into a real communion with other souls, who are linked to us within that tide."[10]

Closely related to this basic conviction is the fact that the spirituality of *The School of Charity* is completely church-centered. Evelyn Underhill taught no individualistic Christianity. Nor did she advocate merely a broad and "spiritualized" pattern of Christian community. Her faith and her spirituality were both Christ-centered and church-centered. Reverently it may be said of her too that she "loved the church and gave herself up for it." She believed in the actual existing church, not some idealized concept of it—the church with all its shortcomings and sins. She loved the history of the church, its art and its architecture, its literature, its music, and its hymns. But she also loved and served the church in its present reality with all its temporal "spots and wrinkles," as the bearer of salvation to souls and to nations. From this "everyday" church, she insists, none of us is permitted to shy away, in order to seek and follow, some more exalted vision:

> When we think of pews and hassocks and the Parish Magazine, we tend to rebel against the yoke of official religion, with its suggestions of formalism and even frowsiness. It seems far too still and institutional, too unventilated to represent the generous and life-giving dealings of the Divine Charity with men. . . . [But] the whole Body is the Bride of Christ, a body, as St. Paul says, having many different members, some of a very odd shape, some of a very lowly kind. And it is in this body, at once mysterious and homely, that the individual Christian must consent to sink his life, in order that he may find true life.[11]

For this "homely" church is also the glorious and exalted "One Holy Catholic church" encompassing all the world and all the ages, both the object of our faith and the habitation of God, where our troubled minds and hearts find rest. It is "the mystery of God," hidden indeed through ages past, but now revealed as the divinely planned living temple, in which all humankind may find freedom, love, and life everlasting.

Among the many beautiful corollaries of such a view of the church, *The School of Charity* gives special stress to its importance for the prayer life. No Christian prays alone; even in the innermost closet he or she is a living part of the body of Christ, through which the Holy Spirit intercedes for all, also when we know not how to pray as we ought and can only breathe in groaning that cannot be uttered. Here are Evelyn Underhill's words concerning the organized character of all true prayer:

> Because of this deep fact of the Living Church, this interconnection of all surrendered spirits, the prayer of one unit can avail for all. We pray as an organism, not as a mere crowd of souls; . . . "I believe in the Holy Catholic Church, the Communion of Saints," says the Apostles' Creed. . . . Here that rich New Testament word "Communion" bears a double reference. For on one hand it means that we believe in the whole fellowship, the society of saints, known and unknown, living and dead, their reality and power, their aliveness, their authority, their witness to the facts of the spiritual life; and on the other hand that we believe there is a true communion, a genuine sharing between all the members of the one Body. Within its universal prayer, thinker and lover, sufferer and worker, Catholic and Quaker, pool their resources.[12]

Such a vision of the larger meaning of prayer cannot fail to give new depth and new joy to even our poorest attempts at petition and intercession. It is not strange that with such a view of Christian community and the life of prayer that Evelyn Underhill gave much of her time and strength to conducting spiritual retreats. *The School of Charity* is dedicated "to Pleshey, with my love." Pleshey was her favorite retreat house, where she often ministered, especially during the later years of her life.

Her final chapter, entitled "The World to Come," lifts our eyes to the everlasting hills of Christian hope. This hope, she says, has two intertwining aspects. On one hand, it rests its sure confidence in the reality of the world beyond, where not only will tears be wiped away, but also where perfection will stand forth in all their splendor:

The pure joy of a keen unbaffled intelligence, of an unhindered vision of beauty; ears that can hear what the universe is always trying to say to us, hearts at last capable of a pure and unlimited love.[13]

All that we call the "physical world" will be transformed. Our limited spectrum of color and our narrow scale of sound are "mere chunks cut out of a world of infinite color and sound—the world that is drawing near, charged with the unbearable splendor and must of the Absolute God."[14]

But the other aspects of our hope is equally important: This unseen world must even now be made more and more the controlling reality in our present world that is "seen." This phase of our hope is the insistent challenge to the church and to the Christian: the body of Christ exists to work for the world's transformation, to bring eternal life into time. And this is to be done, not in some isolated setting of quiet peace and beauty, but "with the clock ticking, the engagement-book bristling, . . . and every new edition of the paper recording some new movement, new sin, new sorrow of the restless world."[15] It is here that we are to find and live that "eternal life which consists in the disclosure of the Divine Charity."[16]

The fullness of the thought of *The School of Charity*, encompassing and interpreting the whole historic creed and applying it to the many facets of the Christian life and experience, cannot be presented in summary form or merely be excerpted in quotation. Evelyn Underhill's own words deserve to be read and pondered, for her teaching makes the creed come alive. Father and Son, Creator and Lord, Spirit and church—each name and word, touched and illuminated by her interpretation, takes on new meaning, awakens new gratitude, summons to renewed praise and thanksgiving. Best of all, as we take up, time after time, our task of spiritual self-examination, we not only gain new insight but are guided with new strength through a renewed vision of the one God in whom all the thought and all the counsel of *The School of Charity* are centered.

16

Life Together

Dietrich Bonhoeffer

*Even when sin and misunderstanding burden the communal
life, is not the sinning brother still a brother? . . . Will not
his sin be a constant occasion for me to give thanks
that both of us may live in the forgiving
love of God in Jesus Christ?*

Dietrich Bonhoeffer died as a martyr in Nazi Germany in 1945—
a political martyr for plotting against Adolf Hitler's regime, and a
martyr for Jesus Christ, in obedience to whom he took up the cross of
resistance even when he knew it would probably mean death. Today, his
name and memory are held in highest honor throughout the Christian
world. Few people are more frequently quoted both in scholarly
theological circles and among Christians. His heroic example and his liberating writings alike speak with convicting and convincing power.

Bonhoeffer was born in Breslau, Germany, in 1906, the sixth child
in a family with eight children. The Bonhoeffers moved to Berlin
when Dietrich's father, a noted physician, accepted a call to become the
first professor of psychiatry at the university there. All the Bonhoeffer

children grew up with academic interests, and by the time Dietrich was sixteen he had decided to study theology. He received his doctorate at age twenty-one. For a time he was a pastor in Barcelona, and later in London. Then, after a year as a student at Union Seminary in New York, he became a lecturer at the University of Berlin for about five years.

By this time the clouds of Hitler's reign were deepening, and Bonhoeffer was forced out of his university position. Totally opposed to Hitler's "German Christian" program, he worked for the Confessing Church and for the Resistance. In 1937 he was appointed director of an "underground seminary," which moved from place to place within Germany. It was his life there, in close fellowship with a group of twenty-three theological students, that led to the writing of *Life Together*.

Under English and American influences, Bonhoeffer had almost become a pacifist. But the situation of persecution and tyranny prevailing in his native land brought him to the conclusion that Christians must also take their part as citizens of the world, even when it means engaging in physical violence. Dr. John W. Doberstein, the translator of *Life Together*, gives this clarifying statement of Bonhoeffer's convictions in relation to this crucial question:

> For him Christianity could never be merely intellectual theory, doctrine divorced from life, or mystical emotion, but always it must be responsible, obedient action, the discipleship of Christ in every situation of concrete everyday life, personal and public. And it was this that led him in the end to prison and death.[1]

The Gestapo suspected and followed him. In April 1943, together with his brother-in-law and others, he was arrested. Bonhoeffer spent two years as a prisoner, toward the end moving from one prison to another. Finally, at the special order of Heinrich Himmler, he was condemned to death and hanged in Flossenburg prison on April 9, 1945— just before its liberation by United States troops. Eight years earlier he had written, "When Christ calls a man, he bids him come and die."[2] Another prisoner at the end, an English officer named Payne Best, has left this testimony concerning Bonhoeffer's last days:

> He seemed always to spread an atmosphere of happiness and joy over the least incident and profound gratitude for the mere fact that he was alive.

. . . He was one of the very few persons I have ever met for whom God was real and always near. . . . On Sunday, April 8, 1945, Pastor Bonhoeffer conducted a little service of worship and spoke to us in a way that went to the heart of all of us.[3]

Bonhoeffer's farewell words to Payne Best were, "This is the end, but for me it is the beginning of life." The text for his sermon on that last Sunday had been, "By his stripes we are healed."[4] Such was Dietrich Bonhoeffer's noble life—and death. There are an abundance of witnesses that in all the turmoil and struggle of his last years, his warm and personal faith in Christ remained unbroken. His biographer and close friend Eberhard Bethge has written,

He was willing to take such risks for civil rights as to engage in conspiracy, and yet he did not simply leave behind him the devotional practice of a long life.[5]

Many of his letters sent from prison bear witness to a warm and victorious faith. In the words of a devout Roman Catholic reader of those published letters, they are marked by a spirit of "genuine unforced piety" and seemed to be "founded on devotional and trusting optimism."[6]

Nevertheless, the publication of Bonhoeffer's *Letters and Papers from Prison* aroused storms of discussion and disagreement as to what his theological views actually were. Especially certain recurring expressions, such as "non-religious Christianity," "a world come of age," and "Jesus, the man for others" raised questions in the minds of many people who wondered whether the great theologian had actually given up his evangelical faith under the pressure of bitter circumstances. The intricate arguments for and against do not concern us here. We mention those persistent questionings only to show that even the most faithful among us sometimes have to pass through seasons of deep intellectual and spiritual struggle. In and out of prison, Dietrich Bonhoeffer was striving to find an uncompromisingly honest understanding of life and reality. The details of his theological views may never be fully explained. But the witness of his heroic, faith-filled life and death continues as a burning and shining light.

During the time that Bonhoeffer was in charge of the "emergency seminary" in Pomerania, he wrote two books of vigorous Christian witness rejecting all compromise in the church struggle that was taking place in Germany: *The Cost of Discipleship* in 1937, and *Life Together* in 1938. *Life Together* has a particular freshness of appeal for us because the theme is an aspect of spirituality often neglected, namely, the meaning and practice of the Christian community. In the church today there is much emphasis on the duty and responsibility of Christians in society. But the distinctiveness of Bonhoeffer's book is that it sets forth so clearly that true community is achieved only in Christ, and it gives wise and pointed instruction regarding the spirit and methods whereby this community comes into being. Completely practical in its approach, it is less a book to be read and meditated on than a book to be studied and obeyed. Taking its stand clearly on the Word, the revelation in Christ, it faces one by one the major problems of Christians living together, and points out the resources available for building true Christian community.

In the close-knit fellowship of the underground seminary, the faults and shortcomings of the individual students—and of their leader—came into clear focus. Bonhoeffer's discussion of these problems and their solutions in a life of Christ-centered fellowship is often startlingly frank. At times, too, we may feel that his prescriptions for living the spiritual life are too rigorous and too structured. But most of Christian life today errs far more in the opposite direction: we tend to be careless, easy-going, and undisciplined. So even if we cannot follow his instructions in all detail, Bonhoeffer's words of counsel and direction deserve to be carefully weighed. They originate in life and are aimed to shape life. Certainly, if heeded, they will inject some "iron atoms" into our flabby souls.

He speaks first of three aspects of nurturing Christian community: being together, praying together, and eating together. Concerning the privilege of having the physical closeness of other Christians, we can discern a tragic sadness underlying his words when we remember the years he spent alone in prison:

> The physical presence of other Christians is a source of incomparable joy and strength to the believer. Longingly, the imprisoned Apostle Paul calls his "dearly beloved son in the faith," Timothy, to come to him in prison in the last days of his life: he would see him again and have him near. . . . Remembering the congregation in Thessalonica, Paul prays "night and day . . . exceedingly that we might see your face."

The believer feels no shame, as though he were still living too much in the flesh, when he yearns for the physical presence of other Christians. Man was created in a body, the Son of God appeared on earth in a body, he was raised in a body, in the sacrament the believer received the Lord Christ in the body, and the resurrection of the dead will bring about the perfected fellowship of God's spiritual-physical creatures.[7]

Bonhoeffer has much to say about prayer, both private and with others. Like the other masters of the spiritual life, he knows that prayer is the heart of religion. United praying, in home and in the church fellowship, is to be both spoken and sung—for singing, too, has a large place in the Christian life. And for the individual and the congregation "the Psalter is the great school of prayer."[8] Prayers may often be formal or liturgical. Concerning the value and importance of free prayer as an aid to the Christian community, Bonhoeffer writes:

No matter what objections there may be, the fact simply remains that where Christians want to live together under the Word of God, they may and they should pray together in their own words. They have common petitions, common thanks, common intercessions to bring to God, and they should do so joyfully and confidently. . . . It is in fact of the most normal thing in the common Christian life to pray together. Good and profitable as our restraints may be in order to keep our prayer pure and biblical, they must nevertheless not stifle free prayer itself, for Jesus Christ attached a great promise to it.[9]

Our daily meals together, too, should be a means of building Christian community. Every meal, says Bonhoeffer, should have a certain likeness to the Holy Sacrament, in which the presence of Christ is manifested. Every meal, too, should have a certain festive quality about it, for through our daily meals God is calling us to rejoice and be glad. This becomes the most true when we remember that daily bread is always "our," never "my" daily bread:

We share our bread. Thus we are firmly bound to one another, not only in the Spirit but in our whole physical being. . . . "Deal thy bread to the hungry . . . " (Isaiah 58:7). So long as we eat our bread together we shall have sufficient even with the least.[10]

The Scriptures speak of three kinds of table fellowship that Jesus keeps with his own: daily fellowship at table, the table fellowship of the Lord's Supper, and the final table fellowship in the Kingdom of God. But in all three the one thing that counts is that "their eyes were opened and they knew him."[11]

To grow strong and effective, the Christian must have not only companionship and nourishment, but also discipleship. Like all the great spiritual teachers, Bonhoeffer gives great emphasis to this aspect of the Christian life. Among its most important forms he stresses three: 1) the cultivation of silence, 2) the control of the tongue, and 3) the confession of sins.

Spiritual silence is defined as "the simple stillness of the individual under the Word of God."[12] By this Bonhoeffer means not only a quiet listening to the voice of God in church or in Scripture reading, but also keen attention to "the Word within":

We are silent at the beginning of the day because God should have the first word, and we are silent before going to sleep because the last word also belongs to God. We keep silence solely for the sake of the Word. . . .

The stillness before the Word will exert its influence upon the whole day.[13]

But if our silences are important, the control of our speech is equally so. We must learn to speak so that our words "may minister grace unto the hearers" (Ephesians 4:29). And the right exercise of speech will be a strong creative force for the building of true community:

He who holds his tongue in check controls both mind and body (James 3:21). Thus it must be a decisive rule of every Christian fellowship that each individual is prohibited from saying much that occurs to him. . . .

Where the discipline of the tongue is practiced . . . each individual will make a matchless discovery. He will be able to cease from constantly scrutinizing the other person, condemning him, putting him in his particular place. . . . Now we can allow the brother to exist as a completely free person, as God made him to be.[14]

One of the most effective aids toward achieving "breakthrough into community" is the confession of sins. Both secular and Christian counselors have known and stressed the value of sharing guilt through confession if burdened hearts are to be set free. But it is, says Bonhoeffer, supremely in the Christian community, the Christian congregation, that this can and should occur:

> In confession the break-through to community takes place. Sin demands to have a man by himself. It withdraws him from the community. The more isolated a person is, the more destructive will be the power of sin over him. . . . Sin wants to remain unknown. It shuns the light. In the darkness of the unexpressed it poisons the whole being of a person. This can happen even in the midst of a pious community. In confession, the light of the Gospel breaks into the darkness and seclusion of the heart. . . .

> Since the confession of sin is made in the presence of a Christian brother, the last stronghold of self-justification is abandoned.[15]

Without confession, Christians are deprived of one of their greatest resources and soon their lives wither and die. But through confession comes a "breakthrough into joy":

> As the first disciples left all and followed when Jesus called, so in confession the Christian gives up all and follows. Confession is discipleship. Life with Jesus Christ and his community has begun. . . . What happened to us in baptism is bestowed upon us anew in confession. We are delivered out of darkness into the Kingdom of Jesus Christ. . . . "Weeping may endure for the night, but joy cometh in the morning" (Psalm 30:5).[16]

And finally, says Bonhoeffer,

> Though it is true that confession is an act in the name of Christ that is complete in itself . . . it serves the Christian community especially as a preparation for the common reception of the holy Communion. Reconciled to God and men, Christians desire to receive the body and blood of Christ . . . and receiving that [they receive] forgiveness, new life,

and salvation. . . . The fellowship of the Lord's Supper is the superlative fulfillment of Christian fellowship.[17]

The pathway of discipleship may at times be a very difficult one: "the gate is narrow and the way is hard" (Matthew 7:14). But it is supremely a way of joy, of joy unspeakable in the community that only Christ through the Holy Spirit can create.

Long ago the church father Tertullian said, "The blood of the martyrs is the seed of the church." *Life Together* is a precious seed left by one of the great Christian martyrs of our time. Its vision of Christian truth and practice, was, in a sense, purchased at the cost of the lifeblood of its heroic author. Those who read it today are his unworthy debtors—and his would-be disciples. We are called to walk in his way, though we may never follow it to the end, as he did.

Epilogue

Like the householder in our Lord's parable, we who have worked together on the inward pilgrimage, illuminated by some of the great spiritual classics, have found treasures both new and old. Some of these treasures may have seemed obscure and difficult to obtain, but some were transparently clear and so precious that our hearts were stirred to "sell all" and immediately buy the field where they lay.

But living the spiritual life is not the decision of a moment; it is the achievement of a lifetime, enabled and empowered by the Holy Spirit. Each heart must possess its own possessions. Things new and old must both be recognized, examined, and weighed; only "bit by bit" do they become a part of the soul's personal inheritance. As all the spiritual classics stress, the heart of this process of spiritual growth is *prayer*. And though the costs of a dedicated life of prayer are great, the rewards are beyond measure.

Of these rewards, the first and ultimate is the experience of a deepening communion with God—the sense of God's presence, strength-giving grace, unfailing love. "Whom have I in heaven but thee? And there is nothing upon earth that I desire besides thee," cries the psalmist who has won his way through deep doubt to the assurance of unbroken fellowship with God. "My flesh and my heart may fail, but God is the strength of my heart and my portion forever" (Psalm 73.25-26).

And almost as wonderful as the nearness of God is the vivid sense of an encompassing fellowship of those, from all the Christian ages, who have lived and worked as good friends of God. In the spiritual classics, the whole company of these seem to draw near until we are surrounded by a great cloud of "the spirits of just men made perfect." Within this goodly fellowship we share the crust of the desert fathers; we laugh and sing with St. Francis and his Little Poor Men; we explore the mansions with St. Teresa; we glory with Martin Luther in the freedom of the justified Christian; with John Woolman we bear the burdens of poverty and slavery; with Brother Lawrence in his kitchen we meet God among the pots and kettles; we think through the glories of the incarnation with Evelyn Underhill. The riches of all are ours, and we are Christ's and Christ is God's.

Yet our final goal can never be our own spiritual enrichment or enjoyment. The great spiritual writers all clearly teach that the coming of the kingdom takes priority over the attainment of even the finest of our individual aims. Life for each Christian is to be found not by saving and perfecting it, but by losing it on behalf of the kingdom. The coming of that kingdom in its fullness—not only within our own hearts, but also in the whole world and through the whole church—must be the constant theme of both our prayer and our lives.

"Even so, come, Lord Jesus," prays the bride at the end of the Book of Revelation. So the church has prayed through 2,000 years, and yet the full coming of the kingdom tarries. But thank God it is not only the bride that prays for the coming and the consummation. Also the Spirit says, "Come!"

Therein lies our true hope: a new revelation of the voice and the power of the Holy Spirit, calling, unified, perfecting the people of God. Many signs across the world today signal a deep and widespread renewal, a new fullness of the Spirit at hand. Is it actually in the final sense, "the time of the end"? We cannot say. But we can echo, with longing hearts, the prayer of Evelyn Underhill, in her "Veni Creator," written for Pentecost Eve:

When the morning wind
Blows down the world, O Spirit, show Thy power;
Awaken the dreams within the languid mind
And bring Thy seed and flower.[1]

Questions for Reflection and Discussion

PROLOGUE

1. What is your initial response to the title of this book? What is the relationship between the inward and outward journey?
2. On page 11, which of the five characteristics of the sixteen books selected here for discussion is most important to you? Why?
3. Have you ever thought of becoming the "companion" of someone who lived long ago? How might this be possible through writing and reading?
4. If there are in fact many types of Christian spirituality, what are the implications of this for life in the church today? Are there standards for spirituality as there are for doctrine? If so, what are they?
5. The author says the writers presented here do not favor spiritual individualism. What does individualism mean, and how do you see it in today's society?

1. THE CONFESSIONS
Central Theme: Conversion

1. Do you know any adult converts of Christianity? What do those who did not grow up as Christians bring to the Christian community?
2. Can you identify with St. Augustine's desire to delay repentance when he said, "Make me pure—but not yet"?
3. Is there someone whom you long to see in the faith, as Monica did? What are you doing about that?
4. Have you ever experienced a conversation like that of Augustine and Monica, in which you seemed to rise to the eternal? What was it like?
5. Choose one of the quotations in the middle of page 20. What do you see in it that enlarges your understanding?
6. How do you see God dwelling in you and you in God?

2. THE DESERT FATHERS
Central Theme: Communion

1. Is communion with God a priceless treasure for you, so that you would give up all else for it? What form did such a giving-up take for the desert fathers and mothers? What shape might it take for you?
2. Author Bernhard Christensen praises the dedication of the hermits

but also suggests that they had missed out on "world-affirming and world-serving qualities" of Christian spirituality. What do you think he meant by this?

3. Choose one quotation from pages 27 and 28 to ponder. What does it mean for you?

4. The men and women of the desert were characterized by love. How does this attribute relate to their solitude?

5. What would you think of making as a motto for Christian faith, "The alone with the Alone"?

3. THE LITTLE FLOWERS OF ST. FRANCIS

Central Theme: Joy

1. What would "rebuilding the church" mean for us today?

2. Can we benefit from legends and other stories that are not historically verifiable? How? What is the difference for today's spirituality between historical events and imagined events?

3. How do you deal with difficult issues of "discernment"? When it is not clear what path God is calling you to, how can you get help in hearing God's call?

4. What do you think true humility is? How did it show itself in St. Francis's life?

5. St. Francis has been chosen by the Roman Catholic church as the patron saint of ecology. What evidence from his life and song do you see for this connection? What form would such sainthood take today?

6. How do you respond to calling the earth "mother" and death "sister"?

4. THE IMITATION OF CHRIST

Central Theme: Humility

1. Is it the duty of Christians to bring aid to the sick, even if it may mean death, as it did for Gerhard de Groote?

2. Many movements of spiritual renewal in the past have not been favored by the clergy or church authorities. Is this still true today? Why or why not?

3. Christian education was important for the men and women of this movement, as well as for Bernhard Christensen. What forms of

Christian education have you experienced, and how have they helped or harmed you?

4. Do you agree with Christensen that asceticism can be worthwhile? What forms of asceticism do you think are needed for Christians today?

5. Are prayer and devotion "good in themselves" without any social purpose? Or are they only justified by results in society?

6. Review the nine themes of *The Imitation of Christ* listed on pages 44 through 47. Which of these seems most important? Which seems most difficult? Which seems most rewarding?

7. What is the importance of Holy Communion in your own spiritual life?

5. THE FREEDOM OF THE CHRISTIAN
Central Theme: Freedom

1. If you were choosing one theme to describe the Christian life, would you choose freedom, as Martin Luther did? Or would you choose another theme? What would it be? Why?

2. What is your reaction to the central paradox of this work concerning the "twofold nature" of human beings (described on page 53)?

3. Does Luther's distinction between inner and outer destroy the unity of the person by forcing us to separate body and soul? Or does this distinction preserve the unity of the human being?

4. What does Luther mean by the words law, gospel, works, and faith?

5. What is the role of good works in the spiritual life, according to Luther?

6. THE INTERIOR CASTLE
Central Theme: Union

1. What is implied about human beings by comparing us to diamond castles with many rooms?

2. What is the relationship between knowing the inner rooms of oneself and knowing God? What is St. Teresa's answer, and what is your answer?

3. St. Teresa had visions of God and angels, but she did not value them. What did she value more highly? Do you agree?

4. Mystics are also commonly thought to be heavenly minded people of little earthly good. How does St. Teresa fit or not fit this stereotype?
5. What has been your experience of the two kinds of "fountains" representing different kinds of prayer, the one of skill and the one of the gift?
6. Does the strength for the spiritual life come from the human being or from the Spirit of God? What has been your experience?
7. Is it appropriate, helpful, or misleading to refer to union with God as the goal of the Christian life?
8. How would you compare St. Teresa's view of freedom with Martin Luther's view in the previous chapter?

7. THE BOOK OF COMMON PRAYER
Central Theme: Psalms
1. What is the value of pursuing the spiritual life in a community? Is there anything essential about the church for spiritual life?
2. What do you think about the use of written prayers as distinct from spontaneous prayers? Do you use them both? When and where is one or the other more appropriate?
3. What is the role of the Psalms in your spiritual life?
4. Do you use a guide when you read Scripture for personal devotion, or do you choose passages spontaneously? What is the advantage of each approach?
5. What kind of church unity do you think is needed? How would it show itself? Which different Christian denominations have you experienced?

8. THE PRACTICE OF THE PRESENCE OF GOD
Central Theme: Presence
1. What spiritual "methods" have you tried? What were the results?
2. What was the main point of Brother Lawrence's practice?
3. What would be some of your activities that would be compatible with Brother Lawrence's practice? Could you use his practice on your job? While doing work at home? In relaxation?
4. Which of Lawrence's subordinate teachings are helpful to you?

9. PILGRIM'S PROGRESS

Central Theme: Perseverance

1. Have you experienced anything like Christian's unburdening at the Cross? Do you think this experience is a once-in-a-lifetime event or a frequent occurrence? Why?

2. Can you recall personal experiences like Christian's with Apollyon, Talkative, Atheist, Mr. Money-love, or Ignorance? What have you learned from these experiences?

3. How is current culture in America similar to that of Vanity Fair? Think about the meaning of the phrase, which is now the title of a popular magazine.

4. How is the experience of depression like or unlike Christian's stay with the Giant Despair in Doubting Castle?

5. Are there good reasons today for wanting to reach Mount Zion among the Delectable Mountains? What specifically makes heaven "delectable" in your view? Or is heaven not a delectable place? How might such a longing for heaven affect one's life in this world?

6. Note the use of "humiliation" as a synonym for "humility." What do you see as the role of humility in the Christian life in a culture that exalts pride? Are there misunderstandings about humility that should be corrected?

10. THE JOURNAL OF JOHN WOOLMAN

Central Theme: Simplicity

1. What are the two characteristics that author Bernhard Christensen believes makes this a classic? Describe how they fit together for John Woolman.

2. Do you agree with Woolman's conviction that Christians should live simply? Why or why not?

3. Is it appropriate for Christians to use their purchasing power to affect policies in the marketplace? For example, should Christians avoid buying clothes made by child labor overseas? Should Christians influence television content by the products they choose?

4. Has God ever spoken to you in a dream? What are the benefits and dangers of receiving guidance through dreams?

5. Have you ever kept a spiritual journal? If so, what were the results in doing so?

11. FOR SELF-EXAMINATION
Central Theme: Discipline

1. Are "indirectness" and "irony" needed today to communicate the gospel today, as Søren Kierkegaard believed them necessary in nineteenth-century Denmark? Or does directness work best in our society?
2. Do you believe in family curses as Kierkegaard did? Can you give an example of how your family history affects you today?
3. What was the role of Regina Olsen in Kierkegaard's life? How would you describe the significance of falling in love for the spiritual life?
4. What can we learn from Kierkegaard's comparisons of the Bible to a mirror and a love letter?
5. What does the "narrow way" mean? In what respects must we imitate Jesus? In what ways shouldn't we imitate Jesus?
6. How do you deal with doubt in your faith? Is Kierkegaard's advice on page 106 helpful?
7. For Kierkegaard, what is the connection between death and the Holy Spirit?
8. Would Kierkegaard say that Christians today are too undisciplined, like the horses in the story on pages 107 and 108? What is the role of discipline in Christian living, and in your view what forms should it take?

12. THE WAY OF A PILGRIM
Central Theme: The Jesus Prayer

1. Compare the spiritual goals of the pilgrim and Brother Lawrence. How does the fixed formula of the Jesus Prayer help the pilgrim? What has been your experience with this kind of prayer?
2. Which of the stories about the pilgrim on pages 112 to 114 affects you the most? Why?
3. How would you define prayer? What is your evaluation of the definition given in the pilgrim's book? How might intercession and silence be important to prayer?
4. Do you have serious discussions about spiritual matters, such as the ones described here? Is it important to have others to talk with about one's faith, or is faith so private that it should not be shared? With whom can you share your faith life?

13. CREATIVE PRAYER
Central Theme: Communion with God

1. What does the title of this book suggest to you? In what ways might you be creative in prayer? Do you think God might find delight in such creativity?
2. How would you define prayer? Compare E. Herman's definition of prayer (on page 119) with your own and with the Orthodox definition of prayer (on page 115).
3. Review the four aspects of prayer life discussed on pages 119 to 124. Which one is most surprising to you? Which is most helpful?
4. Reread the bottom paragraph on page 124 and put into your own words E. Herman's essential teachings on prayer.
5. How does your experience of prayer fit with hers? Note author Bernhard Christensen's consolation to the reader that E. Herman's descriptions may be beyond us, but that everyone can benefit from her words.

14. PRAYER
Central Theme: Childlikeness

1. What do you think of when you hear the term "Pietism"? What is the core of this movement, as represented by Philip John Spener's writings? How does author Bernhard Christensen summarize the essential idea of the Scandinavian Pietists (on pages 126 and 127)? Do you agree with them?
2. Recall the story of Hans Nielsen Hauge. Why is there room in the church both for people with dramatic spiritual experiences and for those who have not had them? What tensions could develop between these groups? How could the gap between them be narrowed for better understanding?
3. Hallesby chose Revelation 3:20 as the key to prayer. What does he draw from this verse concerning prayer? If you were to choose one Bible passage as the key to prayer, what would it be? Why?
4. Paradoxically, Hallesby speaks both of the work of prayer and of the Holy Spirit as the only source of prayer. How do these two fit together?
5. Hallesby emphasizes the childlikeness of prayer. Note the distinction in English between *childlike* and *childish*, the latter referring to the negative aspects of childhood. How could you be childlike in prayer.

6. Look back at the previous chapter, which also focuses on prayer. Do you see similarities or differences between E. Herman and O. Hallesby? What could each learn from the other?

15. THE SCHOOL OF CHARITY
Central Theme: Incarnation
1. Evelyn Underhill and O. Hallesby seem to contrast in their writing styles, but Bernhard Christensen thinks that there is room for both. Do you agree? Why or why not?
2. Underhill founded her teaching on "the principle of incarnation." What is incarnation, and why is it so important for Christian spirituality? Is there a principle that extends beyond the event of the Word becoming flesh in Jesus?
3. Underhill comes from the Anglican tradition that was shaped by *The Book of Common Prayer*. In North America, this tradition is represented by the Episcopal church. What experiences do you have with Episcopal liturgy or spirituality?
4. Is the Nicene Creed, with its focus on the incarnation, important to Christian spirituality in general or to your life in particular? What is the connection between belief and spirituality?
5. Is the local church important to the spiritual life? Is it true that "no Christian prays alone"?
6. Underhill did much of her later writing for spiritual retreats. Have you ever experienced extended time alone with God?
7. In light of the discussion on the world to come, how would you respond to someone who says that Christian spirituality is "other-worldly"?

16. LIFE TOGETHER
Central Theme: Confession
1. According to John W. Doberstein, did Dietrich Bonhoeffer favor theory, emotion, or action? Which would you favor?
2. Is the physical presence of other Christians important to you? Why or why not?
3. Have you ever tried "free" or spontaneous prayer? How have you used such prayer?

4. Review the three kinds of spiritual discipline recommended by Bonhoeffer on page 148. Do you agree with all of them? Which forms of discipline do you consider most important?
5. The practice of mutual confession is not practiced much today. What benefits might come if more Christians confessed their sins to one another? What dangers would have to be avoided?

EPILOGUE

1. Certain themes run through many chapters of this book. Choose one or more of these themes and compare their treatment by several of the writers:

   • prayer
   • discipline
   • simplicity
   • community
   • society
   • surrender

2. Consider the first question raised for the prologue: "What is your initial response to the title of this book?" Does the author intend the reader to withdraw from the outward, or is his view of the inward closely connected with the outward?

Notes

More recent editions are available of some of the works cited below:

PROLOGUE

1. Douglas Steere, *Doors into Life* (New York: Harper and Bros., 1948), p. 23.
2. Dorothy and Kevin Ranaghan, eds., *As the Spirit Leads Us* (New York: Paulist Press, 1971), p. 80.

1. THE CONFESSIONS

Epigraph: John K. Ryan, ed., *The Confessions of St. Augustine* (Garden City: Doubleday Image Book, 1960), p. 140.
1. *Confessions*, p. 17.
2. p. 82.
3. p. 111.
4. p. 176.
5. p. 202.
6. p. 216.
7. p. 220.
8. p. 224.
9. p. 43.
10. p. 255.
11. p. 46.
12. p. 254f.
13. p. 253.
14. p. 369.

2. THE DESERT FATHERS

Epigraph: Helen Waddell, ed., *The Desert Fathers* (Ann Arbor: University of Michigan Press, 1957), p. 24.
1. *The Desert Fathers*, p. 9.
2. p. 56f.
3. p. 43f.
4. p. 160.

5. p. 20f.

6. p. 63.

7. p. 66.

8. p. 72.

9. p. 95.

10. p. 96.

11. p. 154.

12. p. 51.

13. p. 119.

14. p. 61.

15. p. 45.

16. p. 24f.

17. p. 22.

3. THE LITTLE FLOWERS OF ST. FRANCIS

Epigraph: St. Bonaventura, *The Life of St. Francis*, trans. by E. Gurney Salter (New York: Dutton, 1910), p. 322.

1. Bonaventura, p. 311.

2. p. 313.

3. *The Little Flowers of St. Francis*, trans. and ed. by Raphael Brown (Garden City: Doubleday Image Book, 1958), p. 81.

4. *Little Flowers*, p. 75.

5. p. 118.

6. p. 107.

7. p. 152.

8. pp. 143-147.

9. p. 54.

10. J. A. Dobson, St. Francis, *The Little Poor Man of Assisi* (New York: Fleming Revel, n.d.), p. 82.

11. Dobson, p. 83.

12. *Little Flowers*, p. 18.

13. p. 317f.

4. THE IMITATION OF CHRIST

Epigraph: Albert Hyma, ed., *The Imitation of Christ* (New York: The Century Co., 1927), p. 33.

1. *Imitation*, p. xff.
2. p. 40.
3. p. 91.
4. p. 83.
5. p. 83.
6. p. 83.
7. p. 40.
8. p. 180f.
9. p. 90.
10. p. 53.
11. p. 61.
12. p. 86.
13. p. 87.
14. p. 183.
15. p. 114.
16. p. 121f.
17. p. 223.
18. p. 102.
19. p. 104.
20. p. 106.
21. p. 240.
22. p. 241.
23. p. 263.
24. p. 263.
25. p. 275f.
26. p. 230.
27. p. 64.
28. p. 40.
29. p. 33.
30. p. 34,
31. p. 41.
32. p. 92.
33. p. 47.
34. p. 77.
35. p. 52.
36. p. 207.

5. THE FREEDOM OF THE CHRISTIAN

Epigraph: Martin Luther, *Christian Liberty*, trans. by W. A. Lambert and Harold J. Grimm (Philadelphia: *Fortress Press*, 1967), p. 30f.

1. T. G. Tappert, ed., *Selected Writings of Martin Luther* (Philadelphia: Fortress Press, 1967), p. 19.
2. *Christian Liberty*, p. 7.
3. p. 7.
4. p. 8.
5. p. 12.
6. p. 15.
7. p. 20.
8. p. 29.
9. p. 30.
10. p. 34.

6. THE INTERIOR CASTLE

Epigraph: Teresa of Avila, *The Interior Castle*, trans. by E. Allison Peers (Garden City: Doubleday Image Books, 1961), p. 105.

1. *Interior Castle*, p. 28.
2. p. 31.
3. *The Life of St. Teresa of Jesus*, trans. by E. Allsion Peers (Garden City: Doubleday, 1960), pp. 105, 108.
4. Evelyn Underhill, *The Mystics of the Church* (New York: George H. Doran, n.d.), p. 179.
5. Underhill, p. 176.
6. *Interior Castle*, p. 40f.
7. p. 47.
8. p. 80f.
9. p. 81.
10. p. 84.
11. p. 107.
12. p. 127.
13. p. 213f.
14. p. 217.
15. p. 220.
16. p. 229.
17. Trans. by H. W. Longfellow in *Masterpieces of Religious Verse*, ed. by J. Morrison. (New York: Harper and Bros., 1948), p. 39.

7. THE BOOK OF COMMON PRAYER

Epigraph: *The Book of Common Prayer* (New York: The Church Pension Fund, 1945), p. 18f.

1. *Book of Common Prayer*, p. vi.
2. Robert E. L. Strider in William E. Cox, *The Heart of the Prayer Book* (Richmond: The Dietz Press, 1944), p. ix.
3. Percy Dearmer, *The Story of the Prayer Book* (New York: Oxford University Press, 1933), p. 50.
4. *Book of Common Prayer*, p. 17.
5. p. 19.
6. p. 92.
7. p. 595.
8. p. 594.
9. Dearmer, p. 11.
10. *Book of Common Prayer*, p. 38.

8. THE PRACTICE OF THE PRESENCE OF GOD

Epigraph: Nicholas Herman, *The Practice of the Presence of God* (Old Tappan, N.J.: Fleming H. Revell, 1958), p. 29.

1. *Practice of the Presence*, p. 9.
2. p. 30f.
3. p. 11f.
4. p. 34f.
5. p. 35f.
6. p. 19.
7. p. 61.
8. p. 47.
9. p. 47.
10 p. 36.
11. p. 48.
12. p. 31.
13. p. 43.
14. p. 48f.
15. p. 42.

9. PILGRIM'S PROGRESS

Epigraph: John Bunyan, *Pilgrim's Progress* (Old Tappan, N.J.: Fleming Revel Spire Book), p. 256.

1. *Pilgrim's Progress*, publisher's note.
2. p. 13.
3. p. 39.
4. p. 57f.
5. p. 58.
6. p. 73.
7. p. 79.
8. p. 112.
9. p. 90.
10. p. 90.
11. p. 49f.
12. p. 141.
13. p. 142.
14. p. 209f.
15. p. 210.
16. p. 211.
17. p. 211.
18. p. 212.
19. p. 274.
20. p. 275.
21. p. 275.
22. p. 261

10. THE JOURNAL OF JOHN WOOLMAN

Epigraph: *The Journal of John Woolman* (New York: Corinth Books, 1961), p. 185.

1. George Fox, *Journal* (New York: Dutton, 1949), p. 8.
2. *Journal of John Woolman*, p. 59f.
3. p. 87.
4. p. 143.
5. p. 42.
6. p. 213.
7. p. 63.
8. p. 184.

9. p. 214.

10. p. 215.

11. p. 118.

12. p. 82.

11. FOR SELF-EXAMINATION

Epigraph: Søren Kierkegaard, *Concluding Unscientific Postscript*, trans. by David F. Swenson and Walter Lowrie (Princeton, N.J.: Princeton University Press, 1941), p. 542.

1. Walter Lowrie, *A Short Life of Kierkegaard* (Princeton, N.J.: Princeton University Press, 1952), p. 126.

2. Lowrie, p. 124.

3. *Concluding Unscientific Postscript*, p. 544.

4. Søren Kierkegaard, *For Self-Examination*, trans. by Edna and Howard Hong (Minneapolis: Augsburg, 1965), p. 10.

5. *Self-Examination*, p. 14.

6. p. 23.

7. p. 28.

8. p. 29.

9. p. 29.

10. p. 37f.

11. p. 39.

12. p. 50.

13. Perry Lefevre, ed. *The Prayers of Kierkegaard* (Chicago: University of Chicago Press, 1956), p. 212.

14. *Self-Examination*, p. 82.

15. p. 83.

16. p. 85.

17. p. 86.

18. p. 89.

19. p. 92.

20. p. 100.

21. p. 101f.

22. p. 104.

12. THE WAY OF A PILGRIM

Epigraph: *The Way of a Pilgrim*, trans. by R. M. French (New York: Seabury Press, 1965), p. 17.

1. *Way of a Pilgrim*, p. 1.
2. p. 41.
3. p. 76f.
4. p. 112.
5. p. 86.
6. p. 160.
7. G. P. Fedotov, ed. *A Treasury of Russian Spirituality* (New York: Harper Torchbook, 1965), p. 282.
8. *Way of a Pilgrim*, p. 186f.
9. p. 227.

13. CREATIVE PRAYER

Epigraph: E. Herman, *Creative Prayer* (Cincinnati: Forward Movement Miniature, n.d.), p. 117.

1. *Introductory Memoir in The Secret Garden of the Soul* (London: Hodder and Stoughton, 1924).
2. Ibid.
3. Ibid.
4. *Creative Prayer*, p. 12.
5. p. 15.
6. p. 33.
7. p. 38.
8. p. 27f.
9. *Creative Prayer* (London: Jas. Clark and Co., 1921), p. 98.
10. *Creative Prayer* (Forward Movement Miniature), p. 78.
11. p. 110.
12. p. 111.
13. p. 111.
14. p. 94f.
15. p. 94.
16. *Creative Prayer* (Jas. Clarke and Co.), p. 165.
17. *Creative Prayer* (Forward Movement Miniature), p. 70f.
18. p. 72.
19. p. 114.

14. PRAYER

Epigraph: O. Hallesby, *Prayer*, trans. by C. J. Carlsen (Minneapolis: Augsburg, 1931), p. 12.

1. *Concordia Hymnal* (Minneapolis: Augsburg, 1933), p. 315.
2. Joseph M. Shaw, *Pulpit Under the Sky* (Minneapolis: Augsburg, 1955), p. 23.
3. *Prayer*, author's preface.
4. p. 26.
5. p. 28.
6. p. 34.
7. p. 63.
8. p. 79.
9. p. 80f.
10. p. 91.
11. p. 171f.
12. p. 173.

15. THE SCHOOL OF CHARITY

Epigraph: Evelyn Underhill, *The School of Charity* (New York: David McKay, 1934), p. 4.

1. Charles Williams, ed., *The Letters of Evelyn Underhill* (New York: Longmans, Green, 1953), p. 4.
2. Margaret Cropper, *Life of Evelyn Underhill* (New York: Harper and Bros., 1958), p. 9.
3. *Letters*, p. 44.
4. *School of Charity*, pp. 27ff.
5. pp. 45ff.
6. pp. 66ff.
7. p. 67.
8. p. 3.
9. pp. 96ff.
10. p. 86.
11. p. 92.
12. pp. 92ff.
13. p. 104.
14. p. 109.
15. p. 108.
16. p. 108.

16. LIFE TOGETHER

Epigraph: Dietrich Bonhoeffer, *Life Together*, trans. by John W. Doberstein (New York: Harper and Row, 1954), p. 28.

1. *Life Together*, p. 8.
2. p. 8.
3. p. 13.
4. p. 13.
5. *Letters and Papers from Prison*, ed. Eberhard Bethge (New York: Macmillan, 1967), p. xiii.
6. Ibid, p. xiv.
7. *Life Together*, p. 19f.
8. p. 47.
9. p. 62f.
10. p. 68f.
11. p. 68.
12. p. 79.
13. p. 79f.
14. p. 92f.
15. p. 112.
16. p. 115.
17. p. 120f.

EPILOGUE

1. Evelyn Underhill, *The Mount of Purification* (New York: David McKay, 1960), p. 151.